Blasko

Blasko

Better Homes and Gardens®

BETTER HOMES AND GARDENS® BOOKS

Editor: Gerald M. Knox
Art Director: Ernest Shelton
Managing Editor: David A. Kirchner

Associate Art Directors: Linda Ford Vermie, Neoma Alt West,
Randall Yontz
Copy and Production Editors: Marsha Jahns,
Nancy Nowiszewski, Mary Helen Schiltz, Carl Voss,
David A. Walsh
Assistant Art Directors: Harijs Priekulis, Tom Wegner
Senior Graphic Designers: Alisann Dixon, Lynda Haupert,
Lyne Neymeyer
Graphic Designers: Mike Burns, Mike Eagleton, Deb Miner,
Stan Sams, D. Greg Thompson, Darla Whipple, Paul Zimmerman

Vice President, Editorial Director: Doris Eby
Group Editorial Services Director: Duane L. Gregg

General Manager: Fred Stines
Director of Publishing: Robert B. Nelson
Vice President, Retail Marketing: Jamie Martin
Vice President, Direct Marketing: Arthur Heydendael

All About Your House: Your Yard

Project Editor: James A. Hufnagel
Associate Editor: Willa Rosenblatt Speiser
Assistant Editor: Leonore A. Levy
Copy and Production Editors: Nancy Nowiszewski, Carl Voss
Building and Remodeling Editor: Joan McCloskey
Furnishings and Design Editor: Shirley Van Zante
Garden Editor: Douglas A. Jimerson
Money Management and Features Editor: Margaret Daly

Associate Art Director: Linda Ford Vermie
Graphic Designer: Mike Burns

Contributing Editors: Jill Abeloe Mead, Stephen Mead
Contributing Senior Writer: Paul Kitzke
Contributors: Lawrence D. Clayton, Steven Coulter, Jim Harrold,
Cathy Howard, Douglas A. Jimerson

Special thanks to William Hopkins, Bill Hopkins, Jr., Babs Klein,
Scott Little, and Don Wipperman for their valuable contributions
to this book.

INTRODUCTION

Whether you're enjoying the colors of your first spring tulips, relaxing in the shade on a summer Saturday, or watching a January snowfall from the warm side of the window, your yard is—or should be—one of your home's major attractions. How it's laid out, what it's planted with, and what activities it accommodates determine how much you and your family enjoy your greenspace.

In *Your Yard* you'll find out how to make the best possible use of the grounds surrounding your home. We'll show you how to plan an entire landscape yourself, or work out a scheme with a professional. We'll explain lawn care, ground covers, planting and building materials, flower, herb, and vegetable gardens—even how to make birds welcome.

But your yard is much more than just what's growing there—it's also what's going on there. Children can climb, swing, or explore. Adults can gather for conversation, hamburgers, or sports. And the entire family can enjoy a pool, hot tub, game court, or gazebo. *Your Yard* gives specifics about planning and constructing all sorts of special amenities—everything from a birdhouse to a screened porch.

In short, this book gives you the inside story about your outdoor world. We hope you'll find it useful. And if you do, you'll be interested to know that *Your Yard* is one volume in a series that we at Better Homes & Gardens® call the **ALL ABOUT YOUR HOUSE** Library, a comprehensive compilation of ideas, information, and guidance that covers nearly every element in—and around—a modern-day home.

YOUR
YARD

CONTENTS

CHAPTER 6

OUTFITTING YOUR YARD

Portable sunshades
Tools
Furniture
Outdoor cookers

Heaters and pest controls
Watering systems
Lighting

CHAPTER 7

SPECIAL EXTRAS

Hot tubs and spas
Swimming pools

Gazebos
Game and play areas

CHAPTER 8

HOW DOES YOUR GARDEN GROW?

In the spring and summer
In the fall
With flowers for cutting
With flowers in containers

With vegetables
With vegetables in containers and raised beds
With herbs
With wildlife

CHAPTER 9

YARD PROJECTS YOU CAN BUILD

For kids
Planters
Seating

Sheds and more
Lighting
Whirligigs and thingamajigs

CHAPTER 10

MAINTAINING YOUR YARD

Lawn care
Caring for trees and shrubs
Pluses and minuses to think about before you plant

Pest control
Fence, gate, and deck repairs
Caring for outdoor surfaces and accessories

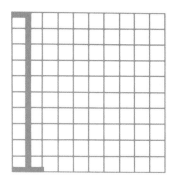

EVALUATING THE OUTDOOR LIVING AT YOUR HOUSE

Take a good look at your yard. Do you see the perfect spot for a dazzling flower garden, the pool you've always wanted, or, perhaps, a wildlife sanctuary? Do you also see grass that needs mowing, clean-up work that should have been done months ago, and unused play space? Look no further. Throughout this book, you'll find suggestions for creating the outdoor living space that's ideal for your family—that combines the features you want with the type of maintenance that suits your lifestyle. Scan this chapter, and when you find an idea you like, turn to the cross-referenced chapters and pages for more information.

DO YOU HAVE ENOUGH PRIVACY?

Think of your yard as another room—one with ample space for an outdoor kitchen, dining or living room, or even an open-air playroom. Then imagine how such a room, indoors, would be sectioned off, screened, and divided to define the area and provide privacy for each activity. This simple exercise is the start of making your yard a real living space.

One of the most important ingredients of outdoor living, whether you're sunning at poolside, relaxing in deck chairs on a brick patio, or tending a barbecue, is privacy. Of course, some aspects of your yard should be enjoyed by other people. Half the joy of a bountiful flower garden, for example, is the pleasure it gives passersby. In general, your yard should be a get-away-from-it-all place, a mini-resort in your own backyard.

Take a look around your house, inside and out. You may find that you can achieve a far more secluded living area than you now have by means of fences, gates, or hedges. Besides adding to the privacy of your outdoor living area, they may help you define spaces within your yard.

Fences and hedges
The view from the glass-walled room *opposite* always includes the pleasant deck, thanks to a vertical-board fence that separates the living space from a neighboring yard. Without the fence, the neighbors would be not just close but highly visible, and the windows would spend much of their time behind drawn draperies.

An airy yet hard-to-see-through wooden fence or a decorative masonry wall is a very effective way to achieve privacy. See chapters 3 and 5—"A Guide to Exterior Surface Materials" and "Building Other Outdoor Living Areas"— for more fence and wall ideas that offer both privacy and good looks.

A creative landscaping plan that focuses on privacy incorporates plantings in two ways. Low-growing shrubbery displayed against the backdrop of a privacy fence is especially pleasing. And hedges of thickly branching trees and shrubs are living fences in their own right. In Chapter 2—"Landscaping Your Yard"—you'll find further information about planting for privacy.

Hedges and some types of fences do more than screen the view. Noise from ground (and air) traffic also can be controlled by privacy barriers, whether you use plantings, baffles, or overhead structures.

Law and order
Before you build a fence, check with local officials about permissible height and location. The proverbial spite fence may be illegal as well as unsociable in your neighborhood. If you need an especially tall structure, a moderately high fence combined with taller plantings offers an effective solution.

Although privacy may be your primary concern, fences and thick or thorny hedges offer some measure of security, too. To keep out casual intruders, make sure gates are latched or can be locked.

EVALUATING THE OUTDOOR LIVING AT YOUR HOUSE

WHAT LANDSCAPING MATERIALS ARE BEST FOR YOUR YARD?

If you were to imagine an ideal landscaping plan for your yard, would it include a velvety lawn, lush ground cover, and luxuriant trees and shrubs? Certainly these elements are part of most plans. But a comprehensive landscaping scheme can do more than just look good. It can also solve site problems, such as steep slopes and lack of privacy, and create a look that reflects your own special style. Choosing the right plantings and surface materials is the key to accomplishing your landscaping goals.

B efore you choose landscaping materials, determine what you want landscaping to do for your house. Do you want drive-by curb appeal? Or are you mainly concerned about controlling wind, sun, noise, or cross-lawn shortcutters? Whether you're faced with the bare earth or featureless sod around a new home, or have a previously planted yard that you'd like to transform, you can create an individualized landscape with a little planning and work.

The beguiling rock garden in the front yard of the Tudor-style home *at right* was formerly a sloped, eroding eyesore where nothing grew well. Now, a well-planned assortment of dwarf evergreens, creeping juniper, begonias, impatiens, and alpine plants adds color and textural interest. The warm red brick driveway and stone-fronted steps bring their own charm to the scene.

This choice of planting and surface materials works especially well, but it's just one of several plans that could be used here. For example, traditional green ground covers, such as pachysandra and myrtle, provide a less colorful but still attractive and lower-maintenance alternative; an asphalt drive, in place of the brick, would be economical and practical.

For help in landscaping your yard, turn to Chapter 2. Then see Chapter 3 for information about exterior surface materials. In Chapter 8—"How Does Your Garden Grow?"—you'll find practical ideas for brightening your garden with herbs, flowers, vegetables, and even colorful birds.

DO YOU LIKE TO COOK AND EAT OUTDOORS?

Dining alfresco is a pleasure you probably would like to enjoy day after day in balmy weather. A table big enough for everyone and enough benches and chairs are key furnishings for an outdoor dining room. But to make outdoor dining truly enjoyable, you also need freedom from smoke and flying or crawling pests, privacy, and shade. Look around your yard for a quiet, level spot with good access—or potential for access—to the kitchen. That's where to set your sights, and your table.

Before you install a gas grill, build a massive stone barbecue pit, or invest in an expensive picnic table, take a good look at the way your family will use an outdoor cooking/eating area. If you already have such an area that you want to expand or improve, or you're creating a cooking space from scratch, consider how you can get the best use from it.

Are most of your outdoor meals hot dog roasts for children? Do you have twice-a-summer moonlit dinners for large numbers of adults? Do you cook outdoors because

it's too hot in the house? Depending on your needs, you may be best served by a portable charcoal grill, a permanent outdoor barbecue unit, or something approaching an open-air kitchen. See Chapter 6—''Outfitting Your Yard''—for a variety of cooking equipment and outdoor furniture options.

You may find a way to use the same outdoor area and furnishings for several seemingly separate purposes. For example, the versatile red tile worktable shown in its shady setting *at left* and in closeup *below* is an efficient barbecue/serving unit when the portable

hibachi is in use. But the table has another equally important function: It doubles as an easy-to-clean potting bench.

Besides planning what you need in the way of outdoor cooking equipment, give careful consideration to where it should be and how it should be screened from general view. See Chapter 2—''Landscaping Your Yard''—for overall planning ideas, Chapter 3—''A Guide to Exterior Surface Materials''—for ways to gain privacy with fences, and Chapter 8—''How Does Your Garden Grow?''—for hedge and other planting suggestions.

DO INSECTS BUG YOU?

Will you be driven indoors again this summer by buzzing mosquitoes and pesky flies? Then this is the year to fight back—and win. Battle insects with machines and chemicals, or, better yet, create an environment that offers them little encouragement to stay. No one can guarantee a pest-free yard, but you can minimize the annoyance you suffer at the hands—or, more accurately, wings and stingers—of things that fly and crawl.

The screened room atop a deck, shown *at left*, comes about as close as possible to bug-free outdoor living space. It lets summer breezes in, but keeps insects out. People can come and go easily, however, because several of the 16 wall sections are hinged for easy access to the deck and yard; all sections are removable for more open living during times of the year when insects aren't a problem. This screen house is constructed mainly of 2x4s and standard screen wire, used for the ceiling as well as walls.

If you'd like a more elaborate porch, see Chapter 4—"Planning and Building a Porch." It takes you step by step through the process of planning and building a screened porch; Chapter 7—"Special Extras"—presents several gazebos that also provide sheltered outdoor living.

Open-air alternatives
Of course, you may not need to build any sort of structure to escape pests. Pages 150 and 151 tell about natural and chemical ways to outsmart them; pages 102 and 103 offer help in choosing insect-repelling devices.

Preventive measures can also go a long way in fighting bugs. Locate outdoor living areas away from service areas where pests, attracted by garbage or lights, are likely to congregate. Cut back bushes—especially fragrant or flowering varieties that attract insects. Remove all sources of standing water and other breeding grounds. Don't block breezes that could blow bugs away. And keep pet wastes far from outdoor living areas.

WOULD YOU LIKE A COOL SUMMER RETREAT?

When the hot days of summer set in, do you become a prisoner of air conditioning? The simplest escape is a grassy spot under a leafy tree. A stone or brick terrace, or a deck sheltered by an awning or trellis, can be equally inviting. For a special touch of cooling luxury, add water. Whether it's a vest-pocket water garden or a sparkling swimming pool, you'll feel refreshed just by looking at it.

You can make any yard, spacious or compact, into a summertime sanctuary. The 36x68-foot lot *at right* is living proof. Here, an in-ground pool fills the center of the garden and is surrounded by a deck that provides a delightful sitting area and by well-chosen plantings that add both shade and privacy. Even the view from inside the house is cool and luxurious.

If your family wants a swimming pool primarily for exercise, and space is tight, consider a long, narrow pool for swimming laps. Another space-efficient and economical possibility is an aboveground pool. Spas and hot tubs also offer water-play opportunities in limited spaces. See pages 108-111 for more about pools, spas, and hot tubs; refer to page 44 for ways to incorporate decorative pools into your garden plan.

Consider habits and every-day needs when you're planning your backyard oasis. Even sun worshipers need a place in the shade some of the time. Densely branched leafy trees are always a good source of shade; see pages 30 and 31 for advice about choosing trees for your yard. For help with building shade structures, from trellises to gazebos to a full-fledged porch, see pages 41 and 113, and all of Chapter 4.

Once you have shade and privacy, you'll need furniture and accessories. See pages 138 and 139 for comfortable seating you can build. To find out more about outdoor furniture and insect-repelling devices, as well as lighting fixtures that will keep your yard usable in the cool of the evening, see Chapter 6.

EVALUATING THE OUTDOOR LIVING AT YOUR HOUSE

DO YOU ENJOY TENDING A LAWN?

Does having the smoothest, greenest lawn on the block rank high on your list of priorities? Or would you be just as happy with river rock and a few very hardy dwarf evergreens? Maintaining a picture-perfect lawn is a time-consuming task, and not all yards—or homeowners—are suited to it. If lawn care isn't a hobby you'd like to cultivate, we'll help you find lush, green, easy-care alternatives to achieving the classic velvety lawn. And if you take pride in a traditional lawn, we'll give you tips on perfecting yours.

The lawn *at right* is thick, green, and luxuriant—picture perfect, in fact. For a lawn to look this good, it needs almost year-round loving care—proper seeding, feeding, raking, mulching, and watering. For more about choosing the right grasses for your region and caring for your lawn, see pages 34, 154, and 155.

If your lot and life-style don't lend themselves to the care and feeding of the perfect lawn, there are several alternatives. You can, of course, maintain it a little less thoroughly and still have a perfectly presentable lawn. Or you can plant ground covers other than grass.

Ground covers also work well on slopes or where shade keeps the grass from growing under your feet. They can be a gardener's delight, too, because they often thrive in just those places where grass will not. Some ground covers prefer shade; others happily tolerate poor soil and steep hillsides. And they can be beautiful. See pages 34, 35, 38, and 39 for more about ground covers.

Shrubs also can work well as ground covers in some situations; see pages 32 and 33 for more about selecting the right shrubs for your yard.

For heavily trafficked areas—under the children's swings, in a dog run, or on the shortest route from the driveway to the side door, for example—think of non-growing ground covers. A few bags of cedar bark or a wheelbarrow load of sand or crushed stone in the right places not only can reduce maintenance but will look much better than battered greenery. See Chapter 3 for a thorough rundown of exterior surface materials.

WOULD YOU ENJOY GROWING FLOWERS, VEGETABLES, OR HERBS?

Fresh-picked corn for dinner. A dining table decorated with just-cut snapdragons. Freshly snipped basil and dill flavoring the soup and salad. These are among the reasons so many people have their own gardens, whether of flowers, vegetables, or herbs.

Gardening isn't really mysterious. All you need to know are a few basic techniques. Once you put in a tomato plant or two and set a row of impatiens in a shady corner, you're well on your way to learning gardening skills.

Whether your main purpose in gardening is to get fresh air and exercise, to gain the satisfaction of raising your own food, or to savor the sheer pleasure of a flourishing garden, you have lots of company in the gardening world.

Spring bulbs are among the most instantly rewarding to

new gardeners. The brilliant red and yellow tulips *opposite* are a case in point. Although some gardeners replace their tulip bulbs each fall to ensure sturdy flowers in the spring, tulips can often be carried over at least two years without serious loss of colorful blooms. Other easy-to-grow bulbs such as daffodils and crocuses thrive and even spread from year to year.

You don't need a lot of space to garden successfully. The raised vegetable bed *above* shows one way to use limited space as intensively as possible. Here, peas, cucum-

bers, and potatoes thrive in close quarters.

You'll find suggestions for a wide variety of gardens in Chapter 8—as well as tips on raising flowers and vegetables in limited space.

No matter where you decide to plant your garden, keeping it well tended is vital to your success. On pages 96 and 97 you'll find information about gardening tools, and on pages 102, 103, 150, and 151 there's advice on controlling destructive and annoying pests. For a selection of planters you can build, turn to pages 136 and 137.

DO YOU HAVE A PLACE FOR PETS AND FRIENDLY WILDLIFE?

Animals, whether they're domesticated or wild, and people don't always get along. When your dog tramples your begonias or birds eat the cherries you planned to pick for pie, it's not easy to think of animals as friends. But banishing animals from the premises isn't always the answer—if for no other reason than it won't work. A better solution is to make a place for your pet and welcome wildlife with suitable food and drink.

Domesticated pets such as cats and dogs, and wild friends such as birds and squirrels, require food, water, and shelter from weather and natural enemies.

If you're considering building pet quarters, or need a place for your pets to run free, turn to page 60 for advice on exterior surface materials.

The two dogs *at left* have an ideal house and run. The 12x6-foot run is made from 6x6 support posts and 2x4 crosspieces. Wire attached to the framework gives dogs and human visitors a good view in and out—and keeps even the strongest dog confined. The concrete floor provides a durable, fast-drying surface. The doghouse/storage shed combination provides comfortable sleeping space and shade for the dogs, and its shingle exterior blends attractively with its surroundings.

Once you've settled your pets comfortably, you can turn your attention to the rest of the animal kingdom. Wildlife can add a special dimension to your landscape. On page 132 you'll find suggestions for establishing a wildlife-welcoming garden so that these visitors can coexist with both family pets and family members.

It's a good idea to set aside one part of your yard for wild animals; it may keep them away from garden areas you want to protect, and it will minimize conflict with pets. If you want to attract birds to well-filled feeders, keep bulb-gnawing squirrels at bay, or find out more about wildlife management, turn to pages 150 and 151 for advice. And if housing seems to be a problem for birds in your area, the birdhouses on page 145 may help ease the crunch.

DO KIDS PLAY IN YOUR YARD?

The swings your children loved a few years ago may be ready to give way to a basketball hoop, or the sandbox to a climbing gym. As children mature, their needs become more individualized—open space and scope for the imagination aren't quite enough anymore. If your children complain that there's nothing to do at home, and they're always off playing at a neighbor's house, your own yard probably isn't being used to its best advantage. Whatever stage your children are in at the moment, we'll help you plan a yard to give them (and you) lots of play space right in your own backyard.

The children shown on these two pages are having a wonderful time. They're playing in structures designed for good exercise, safety, imagination, and adventure.

The circular sandbox *at left* is bordered by railroad ties of random height that make good stepping blocks and hold the sand in place. Ties and cedar posts are clustered nearby to make a separate stepping course. Given a little imagination, the posts also serve as a fort, a castle, or a cave. The climbing towers *at right* offer a whole playground's worth of activities. Tree rounds make a giant's staircase, and a horizontal ladder lends itself to safe but exciting Tarzan fantasies. The straw makes an ideal soft-landing surface.

If these two play projects intrigue you, turn to chapters 7 and 9. Pages 114-117 in Chapter 7—"Special Extras"—describe other exciting play areas and tell you how to measure for and set up courts for your family's favorite sports. On pages 134 and 135 in Chapter 9—"Yard Projects You Can Build"—you'll find a backyard jungle gym/swing/sandbox combination you can create to delight the youngsters at your house.

Plan for growth

Very young children need constant watching. When you map out that first sandpile or swing, make it close to the adult part of the yard. Or plan a sitting space for grown-ups in the children's section.

Of course, what you provide for your children has everything to do with age. Kids grow fast, and their physical needs change as quickly as everything else about them. Consider how flexible your planned play space can be.

The possibilities for your play area go beyond sports and traditional active play. For example, a small sandbox, with the sand replaced by a load of topsoil, can become a neatly contained flower bed, a delight to the adult eye, and a great do-it-yourself way for youngsters to discover the excitement of growing their own garden.

At some point your child may want a tree house, fort, or club hideaway. See page 140 for a build-your-own playhouse that accomplishes several of these jobs.

As you plan a yard that will keep your kids at home and happy, keep safety in mind at all times. Avoid sharp edges, excessive height, rough surfaces—anything that could be a danger. Minor accidents are almost inevitable, but careful planning and common sense can minimize the injuries.

EVALUATING THE OUTDOOR LIVING AT YOUR HOUSE

DOES YOUR YARD GLOW AFTER DARK?

If your backyard fades into the background when the sun goes down, a system of lights, plantings, and protection from pests could change all that. It may take some planning and work to extend the hours of your yard beyond those of the sun, but enchanted evenings are well worth the effort.

Good lighting is at least half the secret of making your yard usable at night. Not only does lighting eliminate the tripping hazards of walking around in the dark, but it can add greatly to a yard's appearance.

Good outdoor lighting is a far cry from one or two bright spotlights—although these may be very useful in entry areas or a driveway for safety and security. Ideally, outdoor lighting is mood lighting. It lets you select the views, lighting up special spots—a bed of white or light-colored flowers, for instance—while more strictly functional areas fall into shadows. Pages 106 and 107 tell about special systems for highlighting specific areas, and on pages 142 and 143 you'll find lighting fixtures you can build, as well as information on outdoor wiring and low-voltage systems that are safe and easy for homeowners to install.

Once you've devised a lighting system that lets you see where you are at night, start thinking about plantings. Flowers and foliage in whites, silvers, and yellows show off their colors in minimal lighting. Fragrance, too, can be a special feature of a nighttime garden. Some flowers, such as stocks, smell especially sweet after dark. In Chapter 2—"Landscaping Your Yard"—and Chapter 8—"How Does Your Garden Grow?"— you'll find ideas for planting to add color and fragrance throughout your garden.

The unpleasant aspect of outdoor evenings is likely to be the company of insects. Using a combination of lighting, screening, or other devices can keep the annoyance you suffer to a minimum. Turn to pages 102, 103, 150, and 151 for help in keeping annoying pests at bay.

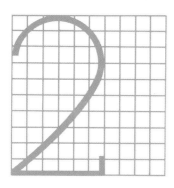

LANDSCAPING YOUR YARD

You're probably reasonably happy with the grounds around your house. A level stretch of lawn, a deck, a couple of trees—the basics are already there. But chances are you'd like to do more. Whether you want to make your yard a showplace or simply solve a few landscaping problems, this chapter will help you get started. On the next 22 pages, we'll tell you how to plan overall landscaping, choose new plantings, and decide what amenities, such as fences and extra walkways, you may need. Redesigning your landscape can be a rewarding and challenging task. Whether you do the work yourself or hire a professional to help, a well-designed landscape will make your home a more enjoyable place for you and your family to live—and more attractive to potential buyers if you ever decide to move.

Landscaping your lot isn't difficult, but there are a few things you should become familiar with before you begin to plan any specific changes.

One good place to begin planning your home landscaping project is at your local library. Landscaping texts won't show you exactly how to landscape your home (topography and climate are too varied for accurate across-the-board recommendations), but they do offer valuable guidelines you can follow as you develop your own outdoor design. Garden books are useful because they describe—and often picture in accurate and attractive color—individual plant species and their growth habits. Garden catalogs also are helpful.

Local nurseries are other good places to visit. Talk to knowledgeable nurserymen about plant species, being sure to note the plants' common and scientific names, mature height and shape, and foliage and flower color. Try to visit several nurseries to determine the widest selection of plant material available locally. (Catalogs may offer more variety, but it's a good idea to actually see something in the same plant family before ordering through the mail.)

Whether you plan to do your landscape work yourself or oversee a contractor's work, it's often helpful to observe other homes with appealing landscaping.

Next, look at *your* lot objectively. List its assets and liabilities, noting important factors such as direction of winter winds and summer breezes, sun angles during the day and throughout the year, privacy, views (both good and bad), and proximity of the lot line to the areas you plan to work on.

A plot plan like the one shown *opposite left* should incorporate the points on your list.

Landscaping can be costly. If you can't afford to redo your yard all in one season, concentrate your efforts on smaller areas. Another way to save money is to buy young nursery stock, which may take longer to mature, but will create the same finished effect. Do not, however, sacrifice quality for economy. Too often, bargain plants are weak or diseased.

What makes a good plan?
All good landscapes have certain features in common. Keep them in mind as you develop your garden plan.
• *Enclosure.* Every garden area needs definition; the eye of the beholder should not wander aimlessly. This is especially important for an entry garden. Use plants or structures to complement and focus attention on one important feature—whether it's the front door or a magnificent flower bed. If you're adding a flower garden, be sure to plan for a suitable background—a shrub border, hedge, fence, wall, or privacy screen.
• *Open center.* A quiet foreground accentuates the beauty of nearby features. An open lawn, paved terrace, ground cover, or reflecting pool can offer a quiet foil for whatever lies beyond.
• *Focal point.* Fine gardens include more than flowers and shrubs. Usually some nonhorticultural feature serves as a strong focal point. The feature can be as simple as a massive boulder or as sophisticated as a fine piece of sculpture. Gates, benches, arbors, and screens all serve as good focal points.
• *Unity.* Restraint breeds unity. For example, use large masses of one kind of plant,

ANALYZING YOUR LOT

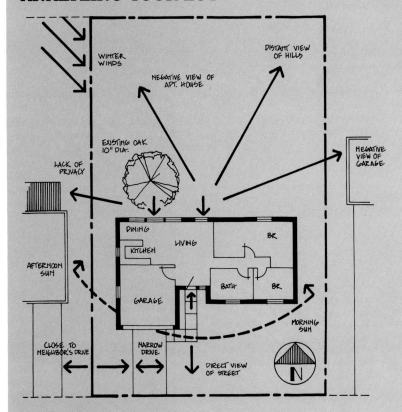

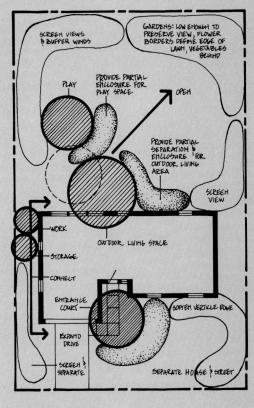

ANALYSIS

These drawings illustrate how a landscape architect might approach a typical ho-hum lot situation. As you can see in the "Analysis" view, the entry has no privacy, and a narrow drive nearly abuts the drive next door. Privacy is lacking in back, too. What's

more, two views are unattractive, although there is a good view of hills to the northeast. An oak tree offers summer shade but no shelter against winter winds.

Now examine the "Concept" drawing. Both planting and structural changes have been proposed. A curved

CONCEPT

bed of plantings adds privacy to the entry, and more plants hide the neighbor's garage and an apartment house.

Structural changes have widened the drive and partially enclosed outdoor living and play areas. Work and storage spaces have also been added near the outdoor

living area. The shade of the oak tree has been put to use by locating both play and outdoor living areas nearby. To take advantage of the one good view, plantings near that edge of the lot have been kept low. See page 29 for a final plan based on the "Concept" drawing.

not lots of groupings of different plants—unless you're sure you're doing the right thing. Variety adds interest, but too much variety can be chaotic.
• *Color.* Too much unity, however, can be boring. A really memorable landscape should be bright and varied. Plant an

assortment of spring-, summer-, and fall-blooming shrubs for a full season of color. Also, include roses, bulbs, annuals, and perennials wherever a bit of color is needed. If you're

short on space, let potted plants brighten your entry, steps, walks, and decks.
• *Seating.* A livable garden offers places to sit and enjoy the view: comfortable chairs or benches beneath arbors, on decks and patios, or on a tree-shaded lawn.

• *Accessibility.* Outdoor living and entertaining areas should be as close as possible to your family room or kitchen. At the very least, plan attractive and safe stairs or paths leading to them. An inconveniently located deck or patio will rarely be used.

PUTTING YOUR IDEAS INTO ACTION

Once you've identified the landscaping problems you'd like to solve or the improvements you'd like to make in your yard, you have a number of options to choose from in actually completing the project: You can plan and execute the project yourself (from start to finish), hire a professional either to do the entire job or to serve as a consultant while you carry out the plan yourself, or do the planning and hire out all or part of the work.

Surveying the site

Before contemplating a major change in your landscaping, you need an accurate—though not necessarily formal—survey of your lot.

First, determine your lot's dimensions and boundaries, information that's almost certainly recorded somewhere. If your home is in a development, the contractor or the architect may have a detailed plan on hand, or the previous owners of your home may have done a plan of their own. Another good source of information is a *loan plat*, a map of the property that generally accompanies the title to the land and is filed at a local record office, courthouse, or with the mortgage holder. It shows lot lines drawn to scale, the location of the house on the lot, the placement of all structures, and any easements on the property.

If you're not able to unearth an existing plan, you can make one of your own, using the techniques shown on page 27 and *below*. On graph paper, fill in the existing features of your landscape— house, garage, driveway, walks, and so forth. You may need to tape two sheets of graph paper together to fit in a plan of your whole lot.

Once you have this drawn accurately to scale—for example, 10 feet on the ground equals 1 inch on paper—you can add new elements to the plan to find out how they will fit in with the rest of the landscaping. This is also the time to decide which existing features to save and which to relocate or remove.

Check with the various utility companies to find out where any underground water, gas, sewer, phone, and power lines are. If your home has a septic system, be sure to note its location, too.

You might prefer to hire a professional surveyor, especially if your lot is irregularly shaped or hilly.

Developing a plan

Once your lot has been properly surveyed and your graph paper plan has been completed, you can start preliminary design work. Determine what aspects of the landscape you would like to change and what plants or structures you might add to reach your goal, using the remaining pages in this chapter as a guide.

You also may want to hire a landscape designer for a consultation about your yard. Paid professional advice often helps you focus better on what really has to be done and—even more important—how best to get it done.

MEASURING A GRADE

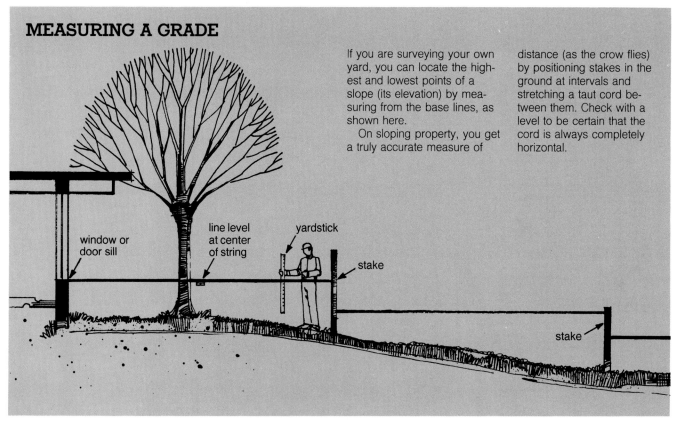

If you are surveying your own yard, you can locate the highest and lowest points of a slope (its elevation) by measuring from the base lines, as shown here.

On sloping property, you get a truly accurate measure of distance (as the crow flies) by positioning stakes in the ground at intervals and stretching a taut cord between them. Check with a level to be certain that the cord is always completely horizontal.

window or door sill

line level at center of string

yardstick

stake

stake

Choosing a professional

If you want to save yourself a lot of work, hire a landscape architect, contractor, nursery-man, or other designer to do all or a big part of the job. Because landscaping mistakes are costly, a good landscaper can save you money in the long run, although the initial outlay will be greater than the cost of a do-it-yourself project.

If you decide to use a professional for any aspect of the work, do some research and comparison shopping. Talk to at least two people for each job you hire someone to do. Get a sense of their general approach and style of work. See pictures of jobs they have completed; better yet, personally examine a couple of their finished projects and talk to the clients. Keep in mind that although landscaping is not as disruptive to your life-style as interior remodeling, there is a lot of mess and clutter. You'll appreciate a job that's completed and cleaned up as quickly as possible.

Different designers work differently, but the work typically progresses from initial consultations to on-site studies. Examine the sketches that your landscape professional submits, and consider the advantages and disadvantages of each. Try to visualize how your family will best be able to enjoy your new yard.

The drawing at right shows how the changes proposed for the lot discussed on page 27 might be illustrated in the final planning stage.

Once construction has begun, changes can be costly, so stick by the original contract as closely as possible, to avoid any surprises when the bill arrives.

GETTING YOUR PLAN ON PAPER

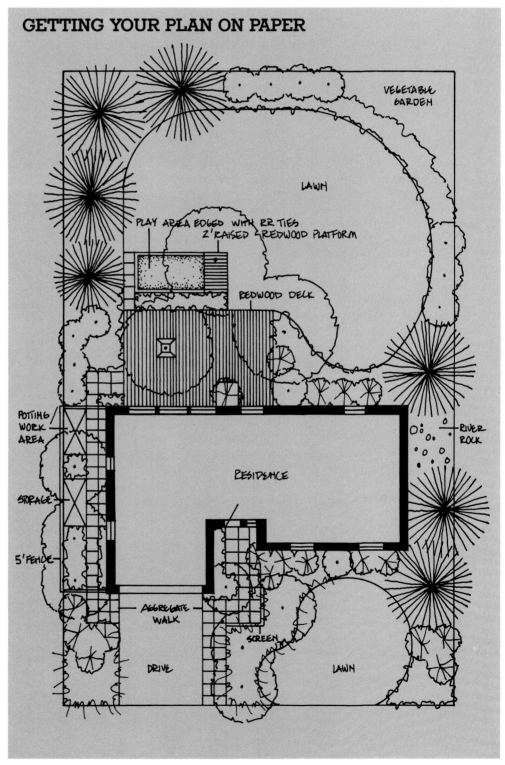

VEGETABLE GARDEN

LAWN

PLAY AREA EDGED WITH RR TIES
2' RAISED REDWOOD PLATFORM

REDWOOD DECK

POTTING/
WORK
AREA

RIVER
ROCK

RESIDENCE

STORAGE

5' FENCE

AGGREGATE
WALK

SCREEN

DRIVE

LAWN

CHOOSING
THE RIGHT PLANTINGS:
TREES

Everyone notices trees. Tall trees, flowering trees, shade trees—all add beauty, elegance, and value to your home. Often, your landscaping is designed around existing trees, either because of their shade or simply because they dominate their surroundings. When there are no trees, their absence is obvious. A treeless lot looks bare, sun-baked or windswept, depending on the season.

Too often, however, trees don't do their jobs as well as they might. When planted in the wrong place, a tree can become a disappointment or an inconvenience. That's why it's important to choose just the type of tree you need and know just where to plant it.

Classifications

For practical landscaping purposes, trees are identified according to three classifications: ornamental, evergreen, and shade.

• On small lots or in beds near the house, you can't beat *ornamentals*. These trees rarely grow more than 40 feet tall, and most produce attractive blossoms or fruit. They are excellent choices to plant near a window or entry, standing alone, or adding glamour to their neighbors. Some can even be planted in a deck well, tub, or oversized planter. Before planting, be sure the ornamental tree you choose is hardy and acclimated to your environment.

• *Evergreens* grow more slowly than deciduous shade trees, but they offer several advantages: They require relatively little maintenance and pruning, hold their color year-round, and can serve several landscaping purposes. The low-growing types fit easily into tight places. Use them to frame a doorway or window—

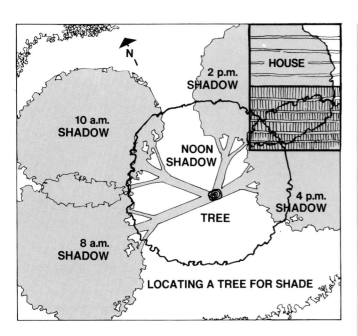

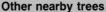

LOCATING A TREE FOR SHADE

but make sure they're not the kind that grow 40 feet tall and block all light or dwarf your entry. Taller species reach heights comparable to deciduous trees and make excellent specimen plants. If you have room, mass them along the north side of your home for protection from winter winds.

• *Shade trees* grow to heights between 40 and 100 feet. Some shade trees, such as willow, catalpa, sweet gum, and tree-of-Heaven, grow very fast and will provide a canopy of shade in only five to ten years. But because these trees grow so quickly, their wood is weak, and limbs may break easily during storms or high winds. Slower-growing shade trees, such as red and white oak, sugar and Norway maple, and walnut, have strong wood and can resist the weather extremes.

All of these shade trees make fine additions to any landscaping plan. They are particularly valuable planted on the south side of your home, where they'll provide shade during the hottest part of the year, yet allow the winter sun's rays to filter through leafless branches. The photograph *opposite* shows how several well-placed young trees can grace a landscape and also provide a promise of shade and grandeur to come. In winter, these deciduous trees let sunlight reach the solar collectors on the roof.

The drawing *above* illustrates how to "target" shade: For summer afternoon shade, plant trees 10 to 15 feet south and 20 feet west of where you want the shade to fall. Large-leafed species like maple or sycamore may shade the turf around their bases so much that little else will grow there. To prevent this, choose finer-leafed species of trees such as honey locust, mountain ash, or mimosa.

WHERE TO PLANT TREES

Ornamentals
Many fruiting and flowering trees work well quite close to your house. Use them as specimen trees or team them with low-growing shrubs or flowers. Space ornamentals at least 8 feet from foundations and 10 feet from each other.

Other nearby trees
Be cautious when choosing trees that will be used within 8 feet of your house. Pick nonspreading species that will remain compact and stay in scale with your home. Use one or two small trees for emphasis; fill in with shrubs.

Trees with spreading branches
Large-spreading shade trees need at least 65 feet between trunks to keep their branches from tangling or growing unevenly. Make sure, too, that the trees are planted at safe distances from power lines.

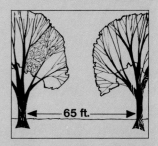

Nonspreading trees
Plant nonspreading shade trees under 35 feet in height about 35 feet apart. Tall, slender trees such as Lombardy poplars (often referred to as *columnar*) are often planted close together to screen views or act as windbreaks.

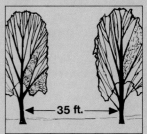

Mixing shapes
If your yard is small, you may want to team a large-spreading shade tree with a nonspreading variety. You'll need about 45 feet between trunks—with less space, the smaller tree will grow lopsided as it competes for nutrients and light.

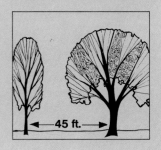

CHOOSING
THE RIGHT PLANTINGS:
SHRUBS

Shrubs are among the most versatile landscaping elements. Their many shapes, sizes, and colors let you select a shrub that is just right for your taste and climate. Besides being used as hedges and specimen plants, shrubs are a basic ingredient of most *foundation plantings*—those plantings around the base of a house that do so much to bring out the structure's best architectural features and help it blend with its surroundings.

The photograph *at left* shows how a low shrubbery hedge can soften the lines of a fence as well as emphasize a dramatic feature such as the espaliered bush growing up the wall.

Shrubs fall into three general categories: narrow-leafed evergreens, broad-leafed evergreens, and deciduous shrubs. Availability varies by region, but within each category there are species that can be grown in almost any area.

• *Narrow-leafed evergreens* are coniferous and include species such as pines, yews, and junipers. They are best used in foundation plantings or as specimen plants. The low-growing types also make excellent low-maintenance ground covers. Slightly taller types such as dwarf Japanese yew are good edgings for driveways, walks, and flower beds. The tallest species, such as Oriental arborvitae and Irish yew, make fine foundation plantings and specimen plants.

• *Broad-leafed evergreens* work well as edging or hedge plants and privacy screens. Some, such as rhododen-

drons, azaleas, and hollies, produce quantities of colorful flowers or berries. For the best effect, plant flowering evergreens in groups of three or more.

• *Deciduous shrubs* provide colorful and less demanding alternatives to annual and perennial flowers. Just one spreading specimen, such as a good-size lilac or weigela, can brighten your whole yard. Try deciduous shrubs, too, along a lot line, in a foundation planting, or as an economical privacy screen. (Remember

that the privacy provided by deciduous shrubs is largely seasonal, however, because they lose their leaves in the fall.) Where space is at a premium—near an entry, for example—use upright compact varieties such as euonymus or potentilla.

For an informal hedge, lilac, forsythia, honeysuckle, and hydrangea are just a few of the deciduous shrubs you can choose from. Privet and deciduous barberry, among others, are easily pruned and very attractive in formal hedges.

HOW TO USE SHRUBS

At corners
To add privacy to a corner lot, plant a shrub border or hedge. (Be careful not to block drivers' sight lines at the intersection.) Tall shrubs like dogwood and honeysuckle work well but often become leggy as they mature. If you have space, you may want to plant low-growing shrubs near the base of the taller shrubs.

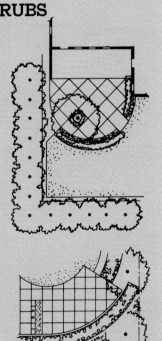

As screens
Medium-size shrubs planted along the edge of a terrace or patio will make a compact screen and help tie the outdoor living area to the rest of the landscaping. Yew, oleander, hydrangea, viburnum, and privet are all excellent choices.

As dividers
A low divider hedge teamed with a taller, multi-stemmed specimen shrub at the corner will effectively frame and balance an off-center entry. Lilac, pussy willow, and witch hazel are good corner specimens.

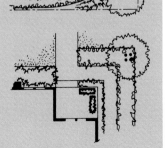

CHOOSING THE RIGHT PLANTINGS: GRASS AND GROUND COVERS

A lush green lawn like the velvety circle *at right* is almost essential if you want the rest of your landscaping to look good.

Before you start a new lawn or try to shape up an old one, make sure that the area you're working with is fairly level and drains properly. The lawn should slope away slightly from the house and be contoured so water runs gently off the surface. Fill all low spots that will collect water. Good soil preparation is another key to a successful lawn. Add a balanced commercial lawn fertilizer as you till or spade the entire area. Work the area until the soil is loose and crumbly; your finished soil bed should have marble-sized aggregates of dirt. Remember, too, that lawns are heavy feeders—fertilize them at least twice during the growing season.

Lawn grasses are generally divided into two categories: cool-season grasses that thrive in northern portions of the country and warm-season grasses that grow best in the South.

• *Cool-season grasses*, such as Kentucky bluegrass, fescue, and perennial ryegrass, grow quickly during cool, moist weather and are best started from seed sown in the fall. For the most attractive and productive results, use a mixture of species. Check the label before you buy a bag of grass seed to find out what *percentage* of pure, desirable seed is in the bag. Contents are often listed by weight rather than by actual seed count, and you may be buying a disproportionate number of seeds of an undesirable but lightweight species.

For faster results, you may want to lay sod; this is done by putting one strip of sod against the next. On a slope,

lay strips across the hill rather than up and down. To prevent erosion, stagger the vertical seams. When the sod has been laid, use a lawn roller to press it into place. Then water thoroughly until new growth takes hold.

• *Warm-season grasses* include the popular Bermuda grass and zoysia grass. Both can be started vegetatively—with live stems or plugs (sections of sod). They also can be started from seed, but it takes much longer to cultivate the seedlings. Warm-season grasses are slow to turn green in the spring, but they thrive with minimum care during the hot months.

Ground covers can provide handsome, low-maintenance solutions for parts of your yard where grass just doesn't seem to thrive. As the photograph *at right* shows, a ground cover can spread over a hard-to-plant area, whether it's a slope, shady corner, or wind-swept open space.

Most ground covers do best when planted 6 to 12 inches apart. Right after planting, mulch the plants to reduce weed competition and increase soil moisture. Once the plants are established, most ground covers need occasional weeding or pruning to keep them looking good. Ground covers bind the soil and spread quickly. There are numerous hardy varieties to choose from.

• *Sun-loving ground covers*, like bishop's-weed, ajuga, bearberry, polygonum, crown vetch, hypericum, dwarf spreading honeysuckle, sedum, moss phlox, and veronica, are perfect for steep slopes or exposed areas. All of these plants spread fairly rapidly and will easily cover a

wide area. Most are tolerant of drought conditions, but should be watered regularly until they are well established.

• *Shade-loving ground covers*, such as pachysandra, English ivy, wild ginger, woodruff, epimedium, lily-of-the-valley, prostrate euonymus, lamium, liriope, and vinca, thrive around large trees and shrubs, in woodland gardens, or in beds along the north side of

the house. They are a bit more temperamental than sun-loving types, so you may want to experiment with several species until you find the one that grows well in the area you want to cover. All shade-loving ground covers enjoy a rich, partially moist soil; do not plant them where they will be exposed to hot, dry conditions.

Plants that are often overlooked as ground covers include cotoneaster, creeping juniper, pyracantha, and ornamental grasses; all four prefer full sun. Low- and medium-

height hostas and ferns also make excellent ground covers in shady locations.

If you need an almost-instant ground cover to hold soil in an area you plan to seed eventually, try a temporary annual cover such as sweet alyssum. In a few weeks the temporary cover will transform bare dirt into an attractive garden.

MAKE THE FRONT OF YOUR HOUSE LOOK INVITING

Because your front yard is the most visible—if not the most used—part of your lot, you may choose to concentrate your first design efforts there and then move on to informal areas in the yard.

Most homeowners ignore their front yard's full potential and settle for an expanse of lawn and a few well-placed evergreen shrubs. There's nothing wrong with this style of landscaping, but it limits your yard's attractiveness. Your goal should be to make this public face of your home good-looking, functional, and uniquely your own.

If you want a natural—and literally carefree—look, try planting your whole front yard with undemanding native shrubs, wildflowers, and hardy perennials. They'll thrive and resist seasonal quirks, like insect attacks and too much or too little rain.

Flowers and fruit trees
Delightful color can come from an assortment of annuals, perennials, and bulbs planted in small beds on either side of your front entry or walk. Use a pine or fir bark mulch around the flowers. This type of mulch is good-looking and will prevent weeds from securing a foothold.

Low-growing flowering trees and shrubs, such as those shown in the drawing *at right,* are also good candidates for front-yard planting. If you plant dwarf apple, cherry, peach, plum, or pear trees, you'll get plenty of spring color as well as delicious fruit. Use these trees to frame your front steps, or plant them singly on the lawn as specimen trees. Other good low-growing trees include redbud, crab apple, dogwood, and magnolia.

Use shrubs like forsythia, lilac, hydrangea, mock orange, or spirea to identify your lot line and make both your view and your neighbor's much more pleasant. Or, try some broad-leafed flowering shrubs like azalea and rhododendron mixed with your foundation narrow-leafed evergreens for a springtime color extravaganza.

Roses, too, are effective landscaping elements in the front yard. The tall, stately appearance of the tree rose makes it a must for formal front yards. Use hybrid teas and floribundas to provide fill-in color between the taller tree roses. And, for front border plants, few annuals or perennials can beat the hardy miniature roses.

Vines are often-overlooked plants that can help turn your front yard into a relaxing, private retreat. Dutchman's pipe, wisteria, trumpet vine, ivy, euonymus, pyracantha, and silver fleece vine are all relatively quick growing and are easily trained to grow around an arbor or trellis framing your doorway. Use lower-growing vines like clematis and morning-glory to adorn a porch pillar or stairway railing.

If you're not ready to rethink your whole front yard, start with just a few items. For example, one lattice panel, positioned to shield your front door, can turn an exposed entry into an inviting courtyard. Or transform your front steps into a welcoming mini-deck brightened with pots of flowering plants. If you have a front walk that needs repair, then consider replacing it with brick or flagstone, which, even unadorned, will add charm to your front yard.

This landscape plan shows
how carefully chosen plantings bring a front yard to
life. Flowering shrubs and
ornamental trees, ranging
from low-growing azaleas
to a 15-foot crab apple, provide seasonal color and
year-round interest. Evergreens assure a touch of
greenery throughout the
year and beds of annuals,
perennials, and bulbs highlight the brick patio.

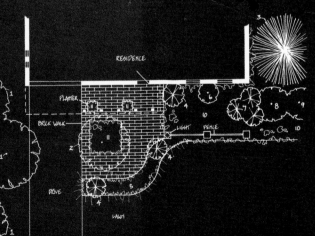

PLANT LIST

#	QTY.	TYPE
1	3	SERVICEBERRY
2	1	FLOWERING CRAB
3	1	AUSTRIAN PINE
4	3	PJM RHODODENDRON
5	5	BUFFALO JUNIPER
6	1	A.W. SPIREA
7	3	OREGON GRAPE
8	1	WHITE LILAC
9	4	BURNING BUSH
10	20	EUONYMUS FORTUNEI
11	—	ANNUALS, BULBS PERENNIALS

SOLUTIONS FOR PROBLEM AREAS: SHADY SPOTS AND SLOPES

A shady lot doesn't have to be covered with bare earth, struggling greenery, or gravel. Lighten up the darker corners of your landscape with shade-loving plants—most of which grow best in partially shady spots, under tall trees, or on the north or protected east side of your house.

Direct sunshine early in the morning or late in the afternoon will give your shady garden the light it needs to thrive. If trees are so thick that grass won't grow at all, there probably isn't enough light for so-called shade-loving plants either; in that case, consider cutting down some of the trees or thinning their branches.

Although the selection of shade plants is somewhat limited, many species produce bumper crops of intensely colored flowers. As always, their availability depends on region; find out which species do well in your climate.

Many flowering shrubs, such as mountain laurel, tolerate partial shade; a few shrubs, such as leucothoe, can even handle deep shade. Use these plants to define a lot line or as a background for a border. Shade-loving ground covers, including sweet woodruff, lily-of-the-valley, and pachysandra, can provide fill-in color under trees and large shrubs.

Flowering or decorative-foliage plants that prefer low light levels include impatiens, fibrous and tuberous begonia, hosta, fuchsia, caladium, bleeding heart, astilbe, primula, columbine, and solomon's seal. Try a combination of these plants along a walk or as edging for a driveway.

For best effect, plant in drifts or clumps, not in rows. Even the best-cared-for plants lose much of their appeal when they're planted single file. Use at least three identical specimens in each clump of low and medium-sized plants.

Some shade-loving annuals grow as well in containers as they do in the garden, as the restful patio *at left* illustrates. Brighten a shady seating area with pots of impatiens, caladium, begonia, and coleus, for example.

You can turn a shady spot into a wildflower garden. Such wildflowers as Virginia bluebell, shooting star, Dutchman's breeches, hepatica, trillium, dogtooth violet, and jack-in-the-pulpit spread rapidly and make good ground covers.

A sloping or hilly lot may bring visions of eroded gullies, unusable space, and struggling plants to tend, but with a little careful planning you can make your problem hillside into a valuable landscaping asset.

The best way to tame a sharply sloping landscape is with a series of terraced steps or low retaining walls. If your slope is small, you might want to terrace the slope by hand, but on larger areas you may need a bulldozer to get the job done. For large slopes, it's best to consult a landscape professional.

In the garden shown *opposite,* railroad ties are used with a ground cover of needlepoint ivy, cinquefoil, and Indian mock strawberries to turn a steep slope into a delightful and accessible garden. Railroad ties make durable, long-

lasting steps or retaining walls. To keep the ties from slipping, bolt lengths of reinforcing rods to the ties. Then attach the other end of each rod to its own short 4x4 support post buried deep in the hillside. Each railroad tie should have at least two supporting rods.

If you are stacking several railroad ties on top of one another, be sure that their seams do not line up and they are securely fastened to each other. Concrete retaining walls should be well anchored to prevent buckling. (More about building retaining walls can be found on pages 92 and 93.)

If a major terracing project is out of the question, rely on an assortment of ground covers to help tame a steep bank. Depending on the climate and degree of shade present on your slope, you can plant any number of effective ground covers, including crown vetch, English ivy, day lily, hypericum, pachysandra, lily-of-the-valley, and ornamental grass. Add low-growing shrubs like heath, creeping juniper, pyracantha, cotoneaster, heather, potentilla, hiawatha rose, or viburnum for extra color and variety.

For a quick, temporary ground cover, sow annual ryegrass. It grows quickly, especially on bare sunny slopes, and holds the soil in place with its deep and extensive root system. Ryegrass does not need to be mowed and will die during the winter. In the meantime, however, your other ground-cover plants will have had plenty of time to become established.

SOLUTIONS FOR PROBLEM AREAS: LACK OF PRIVACY AND TOO MUCH SUN

Sitting in a hot, sunny backyard in full view of four other backyards and two streets is not the ideal way to relax on a summer afternoon. To varying degrees, however, both privacy and shade are often in short supply, especially in urban and suburban neighborhoods. The obvious answers are fences for privacy and trees for shade, but these solutions are a bit more complicated—and more interesting—than that.

Fences

Fences offer the quickest way to gain privacy, but remember that every landscape is different and a fence that looks good in your neighbor's yard may not be right for your yard. For example, in a very small backyard a tall solid fence or wall may be too confining, and where summers are hot and muggy, a solid fence will cut off air circulation. A better solution would be to install lattice panels or wire fencing and let vines grow over the surface. Openwork fences of this kind allow plenty of air circulation without sacrificing privacy. The lattice-panel fence *at right* acts as a fine privacy screen, doesn't block breezes, and presents the same attractive appearance to both the owners and their neighbors— an important consideration.

Keep in mind that your town may have fence ordinances. Fences above a certain height, or fences that extend beyond the line established by the front edge of the lot's largest structure, may be forbidden, so check your local rules. (For more information about fences, see pages 47, 58-61, and 88-91.)

Plantings

On large lots, where fence construction may not be economically feasible, plant a hedge. Shrubs such as privet, arborvitae, mentor barberry, and European hornbeam grow quickly and are easily sheared to any height or shape; if you don't want a formal clipped hedge, let the shrubs grow naturally. On corner lots, try Japanese barberry; these shrubs have sharp thorns that will prevent pedestrians from cutting across your lawn.

For a quick temporary screen around a new deck or patio, try growing annual vines like scarlet runner bean, morning-glory, or black-eyed susan vine. When given a small wire trellis for support, all of these vines will thrive in pots or planters that you can move to where you need them most.

When it comes to shade, trees offer the natural and, in many cases, the best way to shelter a deck, patio, or yard from the sun. When positioned properly, trees will also provide some measure of privacy. Paperbark maple, flowering crab apple, flame buckeye, redbud, dogwood, clump birch, and magnolia are all small- to medium-size trees that produce a fair amount of shade in a limited space. Pin oak, Norway and sugar maple, ginkgo, marshall's seedless ash, and honey locust are good choices for larger lots.

Sun shelters

If you have a small area to shield from the sun, are in a great hurry, or do not plan to stay in your current home long enough to reap the benefit of a tree's shade, build a simple overhead structure above your deck or patio. A sun shelter made of 2x8 boards topped with lath strips, 1x2s, or 2x2s set 3 to 4 inches apart will fil-

ter out a lot of sunlight; space the boards farther apart if you want more sun. For less sunny areas, use 2x4 or 2x6 stringers spaced 8 to 10 inches apart. You can notch some of the stringers so they're easy to remove during cloudy periods or in the early spring when you need the extra sunlight. Keep an extra supply of notched stringers on hand for additional sun protection in midsummer.

The sun shelter shown *opposite* has a lattice-screen roof for an ornamental effect. Vines growing over the top of the shelter soften its lines and provide additional shade.

Canvas canopies offer yet another solution to creating shade. Such canopies are becoming increasingly popular because they are lightweight

and can be rolled up or down, depending on the weather. One drawback occurs when a canvas canopy is completely unfurled—it blocks all overhead sunlight. Also, canvas canopies must be removed and stored during the winter.

Berms

Another method of adding privacy to your lot is to build a berm (mound of soil) in front of your home. A 3- to 4-foot-high *berm* will effectively block the view from the street and add an extra dimension of height to your landscape. It will also act as a sound barrier by absorbing street noises. Berms are easy to construct and should be gently contoured to look like a natural feature in the landscape. Plant low-growing shrubs over your berm's surface for an extra measure of privacy.

AMENITIES: WALKWAYS

Getting there from here is as important in a yard as anywhere else, and well-planned walkways are the kind of seemingly secondary feature that can add a lot to the comfort and appearance of your home.

In addition to your front walk, you probably have—or would like to have—several auxiliary paths to connect different outdoor areas to each other or to indoor areas. A new path might make your barbecue/outdoor-eating area more accessible to and from the kitchen, for example. On these two pages we'll start you down the path to building new walkways or improving existing ones. (For more information about choosing the right material for your walkways, see pages 48 and 49.)

In the yard shown *at right*, garden space has been combined with living space by a system of masonry paths. The colorful planting beds are linked to each other and to the comfortable and equally colorful lounging area by the uniform, neutral paving material.

Not all approaches to the path question need to be so complex. The path shown *opposite* is dramatic in its very simplicity. This long cedar walkway (the cedar was chosen for its weather-resistance as well as its silvery appearance) provides a striking focal point for the whole landscape.

Planning

The shortest distance between two points may be a straight line, but a walkway can be as winding or angular as the setting and your taste allow. Think about your whole yard before you design a new walkway or change an existing one. A short, straight concrete path may work just fine next door,

but an elegantly curved flagstone walk may be what your landscape really needs.

Think about who'll be using the path, and how often. For example, if it's not going to be used a lot, looks may count for more than durability; if there are children or elderly people to consider, safety will be a factor in your planning.

Selecting materials

Select the surface material for your walkway based on the mood of the surrounding area.

In a wooded setting, for example, you might decide to use several inches of fir or pine bark. Tree rounds are another natural solution to the pathway dilemma. They lose their freshly sawn look in a few months and blend in with the natural environment. Make sure you sink the rounds level with the soil to prevent them from becoming a tripping hazard.

For a charming and somewhat more formal look on a path that gets moderate or even heavy use, think about brick. Flagstones, paving stones, and that old standby, concrete, also work well in

most settings, and are durable.

Function and location may be the first things you think about, but climate should also be an important factor in your path-making decision. If you live in a region where heavy, frequent rain or snow is to be expected each year, you'll probably want to avoid steep slopes, narrow, hard-to-clear steps, and slippery-when-wet surfaces.

AMENITIES: WATER GARDENS

Give your senses and your landscape a treat with a water garden alive with colorful plants. Properly constructed and planted, a garden pool requires no more maintenance than a standard flower border.

The key to creating a healthy, thriving garden pool is a good location. Choose a site that receives at least five hours of sun a day. Avoid overhanging trees, and be sure the pool will be within easy reach of the garden hose.

Avoid building a pool that has a surface area of less than 40 square feet; smaller pools are more conducive to the growth of algae. Most ponds should be at least 18 to 24 inches deep. To raise soil-filled containers of water plants to the proper level in a deeper pool, place rocks or bricks at the bottom of the pool.

Materials
Water gardens were traditionally made of concrete. Now it's simple to install one using preformed plastic or fiber-glass pool shapes, or polyvinyl chloride (PVC) liners that mold to match the shape of the excavated site.

Preformed pools are usually made of durable plastic reinforced with fiber-glass mesh. The pools are available in a variety of shapes—most commonly kidney, round, or square. Because these pools tend to be small, they aren't ideal for maintaining an ecological balance. For best results, choose the largest size for your garden.

To install a preformed pool, just dig a hole large enough to accommodate the unit. When the pool is in place, it should be flush with the surrounding soil level. Be sure to pack soil into any gaps that remain between the pool's walls and the hole. The advantage of PVC liners is their flexibility—you can create any size or shape of pool using a PVC liner.

An underground plastic pipe is the best way to channel water to your garden pool. You'll also need a control valve, elbow connections, pipe adapters, and a variety of plumbing accessories. Check local building codes to ensure that your installation will meet local standards.

Miniature water gardens
If you don't have space for a standard-size garden pool, you can create a miniature water garden like the one shown *at right*. A wooden tub or half-barrel, even a garbage can, metal trough, or other watertight container, will do. In cold climates these miniatures are not practical for overwintering fish and plants, but you can keep water lilies and other aquatic bloomers thriving all summer long.

Aquatic plants
Whatever size, shape, and material your garden pool is, you'll want to grow a variety of plants in it.
• The most important group of plants to grow in your pool are the *oxygenators*. They help keep water clear by competing with algae for food and light. Good oxygenators include elodea, milfoil, and cabomba.
• At the edges of a natural pool or in moist soil that covers the overlaps of a PVC-lined pool, you can grow another category of plants—*marginal aquatics*. These are ornamental plants whose leaves and flowers grow above the waterline. Most marginal aquatics prefer to grow in shallow water or along a muddy shoreline. Use marginal aquatics to help camouflage the pool's edge. Marginal aquatics include arrowhead, pickerel weed, horsetail, and marsh marigold.
• *Floating aquatics* are desirable because they shade the bottom of the pool, preventing algae from getting established. Floating aquatics float on the surface and feed through roots suspended in the water. Several species also produce colorful flowers. Water hyacinth, water chestnut, and water lettuce are all floating aquatics.

Water lilies and lotus
The pink water lilies shown on these two pages exemplify still another method of growth—they require submerged, soil-filled containers, as do lotus. Both lilies and lotus are large plants that produce spectacular flowers. In a small pond one water lily will probably be sufficient. The lotus, whose shield-like leaves can reach two to three feet above the water, requires even more space and should be grown only in bigger pools.

AMENITIES:
FENCES AND GATES

Fences keep people and animals in or out; gates let them get to the other side of the fence. Most homeowners use fences and gates to define lot lines, enclose swimming pools, and close off views from the inside or outside. Security, privacy, and simple decorative impact are all good reasons for putting up a fence or gate—and a well-designed fence or gate can satisfy all your reasons.

There are almost as many styles of fences as there are styles of homes. If you want a fence that will blend in with its surroundings, choose a natural grape-stake fence or an unpainted redwood or cedar fence; all of these materials weather to a subtle gray or brown. For front and side yards, where privacy is less likely to be a major concern, try a low rail fence planted with rambler roses or some other flowering vine.

Around a traditional home you may want to build a fence that mirrors your home's architectural period. For example, to set off a Greek revival house, a simple white picket fence might be just right. The contemporary redwood picket fence shown *at left* is an imaginative adaptation of that traditional design. An untraditional electrically controlled gate provides security.

In an urban setting, you might try rehabilitating an old-fashioned wrought iron fence. If security is a high priority, a chain link fence, softened by vines or white-and-green vinyl strips, may be the answer.

Usually, a gate should match, or at least complement, the fence's style. But a gate can stand by itself as a symbolic entrance to another living area. The lattice arbor-gate combination shown *below*, for example, is a striking addition to the yard it helps to define. The slightly curved design of the overhang lends a feeling of lightness to the structure. Wisteria planted at either side will eventually grow over the entire arbor, for a graceful addition to the scenery.

For more ideas about fencing for privacy, see page 41; to learn more about materials for fences and gates, see pages 58-61; to learn about building fences and gates, see pages 88-91.

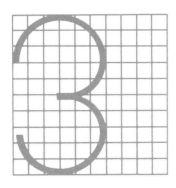

A GUIDE TO EXTERIOR SURFACE MATERIALS

Well-designed, well-built outdoor living areas start with carefully selected materials. If you're considering building, expanding, or remodeling your outdoor living space, the materials you choose will be key factors in your project's success. Durability and good looks depend on the right surface materials as much as they do on good workmanship. On the next 16 pages you'll find a portfolio of exterior surface materials—what they are, what they look like, and what jobs they do best. For information about how to work with these materials, see chapters 4 and 5.

A walkway need not be the shortest distance between two points, but it should be safe, attractive, and able to stand up to whatever wear and tear your family and the climate subject it to. Each of the paths and patios shown *opposite,* along with a few others discussed below, meet these criteria.

Brick, stone, and tile
Brick, stone, and tile are elegant, permanent, and natural, which makes them ideal paving materials.
• *Bricks* come in a wide variety of colors and textures. For walks and patios you'll need *pavers,* also known as patio bricks. Unless you live in a frost-free climate, get SW (severe weather) grade to withstand freeze/thaw cycles. To determine the number of bricks you'll need, calculate the square footage of the surface to be covered. Multiply the result by 4.5 if you intend to use mortar between the bricks, or by 5.2 if you don't.
• *Stone—flagstone* (split into thin slabs), *rubble* (uncut), or *ashlar* (either rough or square-cut)—comes in a wide range of colors, shapes, and weights. Availability varies by region. Flagstone, perhaps the most widely used, is much lighter than most: 1 ton of flagstone will cover 100 to 150 square feet.
• *Tile* can make an elegant veneer for a concrete path or patio, but make sure that the outdoor paving tiles you select do not have a shiny surface that becomes slippery when wet. In cold climates, use only unglazed quarry tile with a water absorption rate of under 5 percent. Three types of tile are suitable for outdoor use: *mosaic, paver,* and *quarry.* Mosaics are sold by 1- or 2-foot-square sheets. Pavers and quarry tiles are 6 or 8 inches across. In figuring the quantity that you'll need, add 5 percent for waste.

Wood
Wood is another highly popular natural surface material that's suitable for walkways under many circumstances. You can create an all-wood walkway or combine wood with other materials; it can also serve as an edging to contain loose-laid materials, such as bark or gravel. Redwood and other naturally resistant woods—notably cypress and cedar—are good choices. Pressure-treated softwoods will also hold up well.

Concrete
Man-made out of natural materials, concrete is the workhorse of outdoor surface materials. It is nothing more than the right combination of aggregate (crushed rock or gravel), sand, cement, and water. Concrete is durable, and it needn't be dull—you can color it, veneer it with colorful aggregate, or break up large expanses by inserting rot-resistant lumber between the sections.

To determine how much concrete you'll need for a project, multiply the length by the width by the depth for each slab (all measured in feet). The result is the number of cubic feet of materials you'll need. Divide this number by 27 to get the number of cubic yards.

Loose fill
Loose fill can be anything from nut hulls to pine bark to gravel. Ideal for rustic paths, some types of loose fill, particularly gravel, are also at home in a more formal setting. More about these materials is found on pages 60-63.

(continued)

YOUR PAVING OPTIONS

TYPES | **EFFECTS**

BRICK, STONE, TILE, AND PRECAST BLOCKS

Patio bricks like those *at left* come in three grades: SW (severe weathering) for northern climates; MW (moderate weathering); and NW (no weathering) for areas not subject to freeze-thaw cycles. Stone comes in three main types: rubble (round rocks); flagstone (flat irregular size pieces); and ashlar (dimensioned stone that is cut into slices of uniform thickness). Outdoor ceramic tile comes in three unglazed types: mosaic, pavers, and quarry tiles. Home centers sell precast blocks in a wide variety of sizes, shapes, and thicknesses.

All these materials are very attractive. They can look elegant or cozy, depending on color, pattern, and design of the outdoor living space. Pattern possibilities with bricks are practically unlimited—choose from running, diagonal, herringbone, stack bond, or a design of your own. Consider using two or more colors. Design variations are more limited with stone. For more about stone designs, see pages 56-59. Mosaic tiles are smaller than the other types, about 1 or 2 inches across and ¼ inch thick. Pavers typically measure 6 to 8 inches across and ½ inch thick, with slightly curved edges around the top faces. Quarry tiles are the same size as pavers, but have angled edges and smooth surfaces. Because they come in a wide variety of colors, as well as types and shapes, you can create many different design effects with tiles. The same goes for blocks, especially if you chose to cast your own, as mentioned with concrete, *below*.

WOOD

Naturally resistant wood like the redwood shown *at left* is also found in cypress and cedar. Pressure-treated wood, containing preservatives injected under pressure, includes many varieties.

Generally, the look is warm and rustic, whether you're using wood to make an entire walkway or simply using it as edging for some other material. For more about specific kinds of wood, see pages 52-55.

POURED CONCRETE

Premixed concrete comes in sacks weighing up to 80 pounds, which yield between one-third and two-thirds of a cubic foot of concrete. For bigger jobs, buy the ingredients separately and mix them yourself or order ready-mix.

How you finish the surface of a concrete patio or walk determines the effect you get. Shown *at left* is exposed aggregate. Here are just a few of your many design options. For color, sprinkle powder over newly placed concrete and trowel it into the surface. To make patterns, run a joint strike over partially set concrete. And for nonslip surfaces, draw a stiff-bristled broom across the concrete, using a wavy motion.

DURABILITY	USES	INSTALLATION	COST
Properly installed, brick, stone, tile, and precast blocks will last for years. You'll have to level bricks, stones, or blocks set in sand from time to time, but tiles, stone, and brick set in concrete shouldn't require any attention, unless their underpinnings give way to frost heaving, settlement, or tree roots. Some tiles and stones are also subject to breakage from heavy impact, as are larger precast blocks.	Use bricks, stone, tiles, or blocks wherever good looks are as important as durability. These materials lend a dignified, here-to-stay look to a front entry walk, for instance, or a patio that can be seen from the street and becomes part of the public's view of your house. For a rubblestone surface, select only stones that have one even face and lay them irregular-side down.	Set bricks on a well-drained level bed of sand, in concrete, or mortar them right over an existing concrete path. Lay tiles in mortar spread over a concrete slab. Like brick, stone can be set dry in a sand base but is more stable if mortared or set in a concrete base. Blocks are best set on sand. With hard-surface materials, provide a slight pitch for water to run off.	Brick, stone, tile, and precast blocks usually cost more than other materials, but durability, easy maintenance, and looks may justify the cost. Price varies by area. Closer to sources of clay, bricks or tiles may be less expensive, for example. Used bricks can offer savings, if you don't mind taking time to clean off the old mortar. And if you have a naturally rocky property, good stones may be yours for the hauling.
Properly treated or naturally resistant wood can last for years. Penetrating stains add to weather resistance as well as fixing a wood's color. To prevent rot, provide for drainage away from the wood.	For a warm look, select wood as your surface. It's a natural for homes with wood siding as well as those in woodland settings. Wood also can soften the harsher effect of other materials.	Wood is one of the easiest-to-work materials. To make a walk, excavate a few inches, lay down a bed of sand, and set your assembly atop it. Be sure to leave drainage spaces between boards and keep them out of direct contact with earth.	Wood costs less than brick, stone, or tile, and more than concrete. The price of any given wood depends on local availability and grade. Redwood and pressure-treated lumber are roughly equivalent in price.
Concrete is very strong. Ask for ready-mix concrete rated at 3,500 pounds per square inch. If you're working during cold weather, request that calcium be added to the mixture.	Besides slabs, there are other uses for concrete. For example, cast your own stepping-stones by pouring concrete into wooden forms, or create a border to contain other path and walk materials. Concrete also makes a solid base for a stone or brick walkway.	With help, you can lay a lot of ready-mix concrete in one day. In fact, because it sets up rapidly, you *must* get the job done quickly. To learn about getting ready for a pour and working with concrete, see pages 78 and 79.	Of the materials discussed here, ready-mix concrete is the least expensive by a small margin. Confine your use of premixed bagged concrete to small jobs. Otherwise, it can get expensive in a hurry.

DECKS

Decks are made of wood. Whether you're planning an off-the-ground deck that extends your family room outdoors, or a freestanding deck that makes a level living and play space over a downslope, the key building material you use will be wood. Here and on the next two pages we'll tell you about the different options that you have within this category.

The big four deck-building woods are redwood, cedar (primarily Western red cedar, although other types are sometimes available), bald cypress (not a true cypress, but in reality a member of the redwood family), and pressure-treated wood (often fir). The first three are naturally rot- and insect-resistant. The last one has a chemical treatment forced into the wood under extreme heat and pressure at the lumber mill. Sheet goods sometimes are used for parts of decks, such as the railings and sides.

The wood you use for a deck has to be both durable and attractive. Carefully check whatever lumber you choose when you buy it. If you spot any pieces that are twisted, warped, split, have large, loose knots in them or other obvious signs of weakness, simply refuse to accept them. Otherwise, you'll have to cope with the wood's problems for years to come. Also keep in mind that stock wider than 2x6s has a tendency to cup and warp, so keep decking lumber under that size.

Most wood suitable for deck-building will weather to a pleasant, go-with-everything gray. If you wish to maintain the red tone of redwood or achieve another color, use stain. Not all pressure-treated wood can be stained, so check before you buy if that's what you want to do with your wood.

Redwood

The standard by which all other deck materials are measured is redwood. In addition to its rot resistance, new redwood has a beautiful reddish hue that brings out the good looks of a well-constructed deck. If allowed to weather naturally, it soon turns a dignified gray. On the practical side, redwood is easy to work with either hand or power tools. In fact, redwood is so soft that it's susceptible to damage, such as denting or an errant saw blade. It also tends to split if you nail too close to the ends. For safety's sake, be sure to drill pilot holes for the nails.

For posts and near-ground structural members, get heartwood redwood (the more expensive grade). For all other elements, ask for common-grade redwood, sometimes referred to as garden-grade.

Cedar and cypress

Cedar and cypress have a great deal in common. The heartwood of both has inherent decay-resistant properties. Both also work well with hand or power tools. Cypress is the stronger of the two woods, but cedar is exceptionally good at resisting shrinking, swelling, and warping. Both cedar and cypress are less expensive than redwood. Cypress is more commonly available in the southern United States than elsewhere.

Pressure-treated wood

Although pressure-treated wood has been around for years in commercial settings, it has only recently become a viable option as a material for decks. You can get both lumber and sheet goods pressure-treated. Most people recognize new pressure-treated lumber by its characteristic green color, but this usually fades to gray in a season or two.

Color isn't the only thing that sets pressure-treated wood apart from its naturally rot-resistant rivals. The infusion of chemicals into the wood during the manufacturing process does several things to this product. Pressure-treated wood is hard, decay-resistant, brittle, and difficult to work. Nailing, especially, can be quite tedious. Some professionals believe that pressure-treated wood tends to warp after it has been in place for a while. Pressure-treated lumber costs less than redwood and lasts just about as long. If you aren't fond of its appearance, consider using pressure-treated wood only for the structural parts and then laying redwood, cedar, or cypress decking.

Sheet goods

If your deck-building plans call for using sheet goods, make sure you purchase either pressure-treated or *exterior-grade* plywood. Unless the application you're considering will come in direct contact with the ground, you won't need pressure-treated materials. With exterior-grade plywood, the waterproof glue that bonds the plies makes it fairly resistant to moisture, especially in vertical situations. Generally, the face ply is either fir or cedar. Cedar works better but costs more.

When using sheet goods outdoors, don't forget to seal the edges, preferably with lumber, to prevent water from attacking this vulnerable area. Caulk all joints as a further precaution.

(continued)

DECKS
(continued)

YOUR DECKING OPTIONS

TYPES	EFFECTS

REDWOOD

Common-grade redwood is fine for framing members, decking, and railings. Use construction heart or clear heart for posts and other near-ground structural members. The latter are uniformly reddish.

Redwood is at home with any style of architecture. Left unfinished, it weathers to a silvery gray. To preserve the classic redwood color, like that pictured *at left*, apply a redwood stain right away. You also can stain redwood to match the structure it adjoins.

CEDAR AND CYPRESS

These woods are generally sold rough on at least one side, except for posts, which are surfaced on all sides. Use construction-grade cedar or cypress for posts and structural members; use better grades for decking and railing.

Compared to redwood, cedar and cypress have a rustic, homey look. Their rough textures, like the cedar shown *at left*, fit in with homes in rural or woodland settings, especially when used with rough-textured house siding. Leave unfinished, or stain to match or contrast with their surroundings.

PRESSURE-TREATED WOOD

Pressure-treated lumber is protected by a deeply penetrating solution. Surface-treated lumber is dipped in a preservative. Fir is the most common pressure-treated wood, but other softwoods are sometimes available.

Pressure-treated wood, such as the fir shown *at left*, is less distinctive than any of the naturally resistant woods, but you can give it the appearance you want with a coat of penetrating stain. Until pressure-treated lumber weathers, it may have a greenish cast caused by the chemicals used in treating it. When left to itself, pressure-treated lumber will weather gray.

SHEET GOODS AND UNTREATED WOOD

Make sure you get exterior-grade sheet goods (plywood). Several types of untreated wood—usually fir, spruce, pine, and hemlock—are available from building materials dealers. Ask for heartwood, as it is somewhat decay-resistant.

Untreated wood doesn't look very different from treated wood when it is new, as the untreated fir *at left* shows. Stain or paint the wood to match or contrast with surroundings.

DURABILITY	USES	INSTALLATION	COST
Heartwood is almost impervious to attack by the elements; common and construction grades are less resistant because they contain sapwood, which doesn't have built-in resistance. Apply penetrating oil stain/sealer to protect the wood further.	You can use redwood for all parts of a deck, but to save money, you may want to buy it only for parts that show.	Bolt framing members together, using washers to protect the wood and to secure the bolts. When laying the decking, allow from ⅛ to ¼ inch between boards for drainage. Drill holes near the ends of boards to prevent splitting.	Even though it's the most costly deck option, redwood pays for itself in terms of longevity and good looks. Clear heartwood is the best and most expensive grade; common grade is the least expensive.
Cedar and cypress heartwood, like redwood, possess natural resistance to rot. Because of their greater densities, they're also somewhat stronger than redwood. Compared to pressure-treated wood, however, their shock resistance is quite low.	Cedar and cypress can be both structural and ornamental. For decking, it's best to use boards that have been surfaced on all sides. If you buy the rough-on-one-side type, be sure to turn the rough side down.	See the installation tips given for redwood.	Considerably less expensive than redwood, cedar and cypress are good budget-cutting alternatives to consider, especially in regions far from the West Coast.
Manufacturers say that pressure-treated wood will stand up as long as naturally rot-resistant wood. It's much denser and therefore heavier and stronger than any of the competition.	In situations that require exceptional structural strength, you may want to use pressure-treated lumber rather than redwood, cypress, or cedar. It's also an ideal selection if the members will be in constant contact with water.	Be sure to have some sharp cutting tools on hand when working with this wood. It's exceptionally hard to cut and difficult to drive nails into. You may find that drilling a pilot hole for each nail is the smart thing to do.	True pressure-treated lumber is somewhat less expensive than redwood. If you find some that's appreciably less expensive, you may be looking at some surface-treated lumber, which isn't as good.
Untreated fir is by far the least durable of your options—at best, it is marginally rot-resistant. Apply a preservative to all surfaces. Don't use untreated lumber or sheet goods at or near ground level, as moisture and insects will quickly destroy the wood.	Untreated wood isn't a good choice for decking that will be completely exposed to weather, but you might choose it for a protected location, such as for porch flooring or—in the case of sheet goods—for vertical applications such as built-in storage units.	Before installing untreated wood, coat all surfaces and edges with preservative. After installation, treat all parts that have been sawed or otherwise deprived of their protective coating.	Although the least expensive decking material, untreated wood isn't a very good buy. You may need to replace or repair the deck sooner if you use untreated wood. Exterior-grade sheet goods are a durable, economical alternative to solid lumber.

WALLS AND FENCES

Walls and fences confine, define, tame, and protect. Walls are generally masonry, while fences are wood, metal, or a combination of the two. On this and the next three pages, you'll discover a wide variety of wall and fence options, from store-bought picket fencing to businesslike chain link.

Walls are defined according to two broad categories: *screen walls*, which could just as easily be called masonry fences, and *retaining walls*, the type that hold back a slope and prevent erosion. If you're considering fashioning a retaining wall, your choices are limited to strong, heavy materials such as concrete, bricks, blocks, stone, and heavy-duty timbers such as railroad ties. For screen walls and fences, you have many more alternatives to choose from.

Walls
Regardless of their appearance, walls need to be strong.
● *Concrete* serves as the foundation material for well-made masonry walls, as well as the primary material in poured concrete walls. Concrete footings, to be long-lasting, should be at or below the frost line, which varies by locale. Reinforce poured concrete walls used as retaining walls with metal reinforcing rods.

To determine your concrete needs, multiply the length by the width by the depth of the area in feet, and divide the result by 27. This tells you the number of *cubic yards* of concrete you need to order.
● *Brick, decorative block, and stone* rank high on the list of popular wall-building materials. Stone and brick walls are particularly dressy. Brick and decorative block walls must be supported by concrete footings, whereas stone walls can be laid with or without mortar.

To estimate your needs for a two-tier brick wall, using modular brick, figure 14 bricks per square foot. For stone walls, use this formula: 1 ton rubble equals 12 square feet; 1 ton ashlar equals 18 square feet. For decorative blocks, multiply the length and width in inches of each block and divide the result by 144. Now divide this number into the number of square feet in the wall.
● *Timbers*—creosote-saturated railroad ties or pressure-treated earth retainers—make excellent retaining walls. They're a warm alternative to the cold gray color and bland texture of ordinary concrete. Railroad ties generally measure 8 or more feet long and at least 5 inches across in the smallest dimension. If possible, buy used railroad ties, as they have spike holes on either end. These holes make it easy for you to drive reinforcing rods through the ties and into the ground to stabilize them. Ties or other timbers that aren't anchored well will move out of position in a short time.

Fences
Though fences must be strong enough to withstand weather and some wear and tear, their function is largely symbolic rather than physical.
● *Wood* fences are available in an unlimited number of styles and configurations, as the photographs *opposite* illustrate, but all of them have posts and rails, most have screening, and many also have gates. To make sure your fence will last, use only redwood, cedar, cypress, or pressure-treated wood.

If you decide to use sheet goods, be sure to purchase exterior-grade plywood, which has waterproof glue holding the plies together. Also be sure to seal the edges of the plywood well.

Prefab fences, such as lengths of picketing, trelliswork, or stockade, vary in both price and quality. Use prefab fences when you're in a hurry for a privacy screen or property divider.
● *Metal* fences, though they lack the warmth and versatility of the wooden variety, are useful and popular. Chain-link fence fabric is available in the following heights: 36, 42, 48, 60, and 72 inches. Welded-wire fabric is available in all but the 42-inch height. You can purchase either chain-link or welded-wire fabric in galvanized steel or in green vinyl-coated steel. To soften the look of the metal, you can buy colored plastic slats designed to be woven through the fabric for privacy.

When figuring the cost of chain-link or welded-wire fences, it's important to include the cost of posts and fittings. These items can add appreciably to the cost of the project.

Corrugated metal has certain fencing uses, too, if you want solid screening for privacy. Corrugated metal is available in unfinished galvanized metal and in several colors in 24-inch widths. This material is manufactured in various lengths that you put together to achieve the overall length you require. You'll need a sharp metal-cutting blade to work effectively with the corrugated metal.
● *Fiber-glass-reinforced plastic* for exterior use looks a lot like corrugated sheet metal; flat sheets also are available. The plastic comes in a variety of colors, thicknesses, and sizes, is cut with an ordinary saw, and makes a good privacy screen.

(continued)

WALLS AND FENCES
(continued)

YOUR WALL AND FENCING OPTIONS

TYPES	EFFECTS

BRICK, STONE, AND DECORATIVE BLOCKS

Sedimentary rocks, such as sandstone and limestone; metamorphic rocks, such as schist and gneiss; and igneous rocks, including granite. Bricks come in varying degrees of weather resistance. Decorative blocks come in different shapes, colors, and sizes.

Stone can be very formal and yet equally at home in rural settings. Rubble stone, laid without mortar as in the wall shown *at left,* has a casual, country look; ashlar or straight-edged flagstone is more regular in appearance. Brick is highly versatile. Decorative blocks, however, look best in contemporary settings. They offer a wide range of shapes and colors.

WOOD

Wood includes railroad ties, timbers, posts, dimension lumber, and boards. Railroad ties are dipped in creosote. Retaining and landscape timbers are usually pressure-treated; landscape timbers are smaller than retaining timbers and are used primarily for landscaping and fence posts, not holding back earth. Posts have uniform dimensions—4x4 or 6x6, for example—and provide vertical support. Dimension lumber—2x4s and 2x6s, for example—are typically used for rails. Boards—1x4s, 1x6s, 1x8s—often serve as screening.

Like other wood materials, timbers and railroad ties have a warm look. In a retaining wall, they provide strength without the cool appearance of concrete; in divider walls, they are less formal than brick or stone. Railroad ties, like the ones shown *at upper left,* look more rustic than timbers. Posts can be entirely covered by screening, or they can become prominent design elements, such as the turned posts in an old-fashioned picket fence. Dimension lumber and boards allow a wide variety of design effects. Space them to gain ventilation and partial privacy, or butt them tightly, as shown *at lower left,* for the visual solidity of a brick wall. As an alternative, you could use plywood siding.

METAL

Screening is either chain link or welded wire; sheeting is solid corrugated metal. Screening comes vinyl covered or galvanized; sheeting is galvanized or enamel covered. Now steel or aluminum, metal fences used to be wrought iron.

Except for decorative wrought-iron fencing, metal has a starker appearance than wood or stone, so metal isn't the best choice unless you're interested strictly in function. Some manufacturers have tried to make metal fencing more decorative by covering the bare metal with colored vinyl, as in the case of chain-link fencing, and with baked enamel finishes in attractive colors.

DURABILITY	USES	INSTALLATION	COST
Stone is one of the most durable building materials. Brick also is long-lasting. Decorative hollow blocks are less durable but, if used as a core for stone or brick, will be protected from weathering and possible breakage.	Use stone for both freestanding and retaining walls; use bricks and blocks for freestanding walls.	Be sure to slope freestanding walls built without mortar so the top is 2 to 3 inches narrower than the bottom. Stone retaining walls should be stair-stepped back toward the earth being retained.	What you pay for stone and brick depends on how far you live from quarries or clay pits. Generally, stone and brick walls are expensive. Blocks are cheaper.
Redwood, cedar, and cypress heartwood are remarkably durable and can be used as is. Any other wood that comes into direct contact with the earth, or near it—such as the lower rails of fences—should be pressure-treated. Higher-up elements can be surface-treated. The durability of any wood fence depends upon how well it's anchored to the ground. Preferably, posts should be set in concrete, in holes deeper than the frost line.	Wood can be used in numerous ways—from purely decorative fencing around a flower garden to massive retainers of earth. Angle vertical louvers to catch or buffer prevailing breezes, create fast, economical privacy with a kit-form stockade, or simply mark your property lines with rustic rail fencing.	Building a wood fence is simple, often satisfying work. First you set the posts, then run rails, and put up the screening, as explained on pages 88 to 91. Sawing several hundred boards for screening can be tedious, however; ask your lumber supplier to cut them for you. Unlike fence components, ties are too heavy for one person to handle safely; ask a friend to help. Also, arrange the ties so you don't have much cutting to do. A chain saw works, but expect a very dull chain when you're done.	The cost of wood varies greatly according to what types you select, but generally, a wood fence will be less expensive than a masonry wall and more expensive than metal fencing. Even railroad ties and timbers don't really cost very much per tie. Retaining timbers cost more than railroad ties of a similar size, however. Landscape timbers cost a great deal more than either of the other two, and you get far less material. It's best to save landscape timbers for decorative purposes.
Both screening and sheeting hold up well to the weather, but neither is inherently strong unless fortified by a suitable framework.	Metal screening—both chain link and welded wire—makes excellent fencing material. Sheeting can be used as fencing or—in its heavier, corrugated versions—as material for retaining walls.	An appropriate framework is essential to satisfactory installation. Chain-link and welded-wire screening, for example, must be stretched tightly, and sheeting must be backed with wood. Wear gloves to protect against cuts when working with either metal.	If you are willing to do the work yourself, the cost of erecting a metal fence or wall is fairly reasonable. Even professionally installed chain-link fencing isn't a high-cost item.

A GUIDE TO EXTERIOR SURFACE MATERIALS

SERVICE AREAS AND DRIVEWAYS

Service areas are almost always purely functional. Whether set aside for storing play equipment, holding garbage, or potting plants, service areas deserve your time and attention. They can be difficult to deal with, though, because they're often areas you'd rather downplay. You want them to be efficient but not noticeable. Driveways have all of the above requirements, except you can't help but notice them. Whether you like it or not, driveways play a major role in defining your home's curb appeal.

For a drive or service area to be truly serviceable, it needs an adequate surface—one that's firm, with good footing, not prone to puddles, and not excessively slippery when wet. You'll also want a surface that's solid and easily cleared of snow, leaves, grass clippings, and other things that might otherwise be tracked into the house.

Asphalt and concrete
For service areas that get heavy use—notably driveways—asphalt and concrete are the most popular choices. Properly installed, concrete lasts for years with little attention, and asphalt requires only an occasional sealing. Especially consider these materials for areas where you need a smooth, cleanable surface, such as basketball courts, dog runs, and utility zones.

Asphalt and concrete needn't look blank and featureless, either. Both can be colored with special pigments and edged with other materials, such as wood, stones, or brick. Concrete also lends itself to custom surfacing or combining with stone or aggregate as in the two photographs, *opposite, top.*

For a driveway or large service area, order concrete or asphalt to be delivered by truck. Determine the length, width, and depth of coverage you need, and the supplier will bring the correct amount.

Unlike concrete, which is sold by the cubic yard, asphalt is priced by the ton. A ton of asphalt spread 2 inches thick will cover approximately 100 square feet.

Note that a concrete or asphalt driveway needs to be considerably thicker than patios or service areas. If heavy trucks will frequent a concrete drive, it should be 6 to 8 inches thick; pickups and cars need only 4 inches. For asphalt drives, 2 to 3 inches will suffice. Both concrete and asphalt must be laid over a sand footing; grading is often necessary.

Loose fill
Loose materials that go directly from a bag, wheelbarrow, or truck to the surface you want covered have many virtues. They drain well, easily conform to the earth's contours and irregular shapes, and—depending on your choice of fill—can be very economical. Loose fill makes special sense for children's play areas, borders around planting beds, and short, level driveways.

But loose fill has some drawbacks. It's prone to erosion, sticks to shoes and is carried indoors, and needs to be replenished periodically. Also, loose-fill materials tend to overflow their boundaries unless confined by curbing.

A partial listing of loose-fill options includes: bark (especially fir and redwood); rounded stone (such as pebbles, river rock, and pea gravel); fine-textured materials (such as sand or finely crushed rock and gravel); nutshells (notably walnut); crushed seashells; and pine straw.

Gravel and stone are available in several different forms. River rock is a favorite service area medium, as is crushed limestone. You can get almost any size of gravel or stone, from pea-size stones to 1¾- to 2-inch rocks.

When ordering loose fill for anything but a very small job, you'll be dealing in tons. Your supplier will tell you how much you need if you give the basic dimensions—width, length, and thickness. For small jobs, you can buy loose fill by the bag, though this can become quite expensive if you need very many.

Volcanic rock and bark are also considered loose fill. Used primarily as decorative accent materials by landscapers, they can be just the right solution for your service area situation. They're sold by the bag; volcanic rock is available by the ton also. Like sand, these materials should be bordered so they don't spread out of their area.

Brick, stone, and wood
Brick, stone, and wood are so attractive that they're not always thought of as service area materials. They rival any of the materials discussed above in durability and cleanability, however, and can blend smoothly with the overall appearance of your yard or house. Bricks laid loosely in sand, for example, provide a solid footing in the rustic vegetable garden shown *opposite below*. Wood duck boards can make a handsome, easily hosed-down platform for garbage cans. And flagstones left over from a path or patio project could add elegance to almost any service area. For a more complete discussion of brick, stone, and wood, see pages 48-55.

(continued)

A GUIDE TO
EXTERIOR
SURFACE
MATERIALS

**SERVICE
AREAS AND
DRIVEWAYS**
(continued)

YOUR SERVICE AREA OPTIONS

TYPES	EFFECTS

ASPHALT AND CONCRETE

Asphalt is a mixture of gravel and a crude-oil extract binder. You don't have much control over the type you get. Concrete is a mixture of cement, gravel, sand, and water. You can make your own or buy ready-mix.

When first installed, asphalt is black. As it wears, it turns to a medium gray. Compared with some other materials, asphalt doesn't offer many decorative options, though it can be tinted. Concrete is more visually versatile, but for a service area its appearance is less important than its durability. (See pages 50 and 51 for ways to vary concrete's appearance.)

LOOSE FILL: MINERAL

Crushed rock, volcanic rock, river rock, pebbles, pea gravel, and sand—listed roughly in descending order of size— vary widely in availability from one region to another. Sand is the most commonly found loose fill, and you can use any of the available grades. All mineral loose fills can be purchased by the bag or by the truckload.

Rock, whether it's been crushed, polished by water, or thrown molten from a volcano, gives you quite a lot of design flexibility and typically has a more formal appearance than most other loose fills. Colors vary from the almost bone-white gravel shown *at upper left* to dark gray; blue and green tones are also available. River rock is less dressy than either crushed or lightweight rock. For uniformity, use the same crushed rock for service areas that you use for walks. Sand is usually the neutral tan color shown *at lower left*, but you also may be able to select white and a limited range of other colors. Sand has little textural interest, but again, as with asphalt and concrete, function may be more important to you than looks.

LOOSE FILL: ORGANIC

Bark—most often from cedar, fir, and redwood trees—is a favorite of landscape designers. Cedar stands up especially well to moisture. Pine straw, wood chips, and nutshells are also popular.

Bark, wood chips, and nutshells all add a rustic, informal look and interesting texture to lightly used service areas. Because organic materials soak up moisture and shift easily, they are not ideal for heavily trafficked zones. Again, which material you choose depends on what's available in your region.

DURABILITY	USES	INSTALLATION	COST
If they're installed correctly, both concrete and asphalt are extremely durable. Make sure that you seal asphalt shortly after it is laid, and every couple of years thereafter.	Both asphalt and concrete are strong enough to be used as driveway surfaces. You can also use them for almost any other service area.	For small jobs, buy bags of asphalt and lay it yourself. Have professionals lay larger expanses. You can pour concrete yourself, mixing small amounts in a wheelbarrow and larger batches in a power mixer. For big jobs, purchase ready-mix.	Having asphalt installed will cost roughly the same as laying concrete yourself. Both initially cost more than mineral loose fills, but last longer, with less maintenance.
As long as you contain them, mineral loose fills will last indefinitely, although you may have to replenish them occasionally. To keep loose fill good-looking, just give it an occasional light raking; to keep sand from blowing away, dampen it during long dry spells.	Loose fill also works well for curved or irregularly shaped areas and over lightly rolling terrain. On steeper grades, erosion can be a problem. Keep in mind that just about all loose fill is difficult to clear in snowy weather. Consider using mineral loose fills for garbage container areas.	Because you needn't do any mixing or extensive grading, mineral loose-fill materials are much easier to work than asphalt or concrete. The key to a successful installation is to provide a framework for the fill. You can use any of a number of materials for a border, including pressure-treated wood, bricks, blocks, stone, or even earth, if you excavate. Lay polyethylene film down beforehand.	Sand is usually the least expensive mineral loose fill, mainly because there's easy access to it in most areas. The price of other loose fill depends on regional availability. You can cut the cost if you pick up material from the dealer rather than have it delivered. Most dealers sell rock materials by the ton. If your project calls for very little material, it may be less expensive to buy what you need by the bag.
All organic loose fills eventually decompose, though most last a long time. Because they are lightweight, you may occasionally have to gather up scattered pieces and toss them back into their confines.	If you're looking for something a bit out of the ordinary, spread a layer of bark, wood chips, or nutshells as the surface for a play or garden service area.	Like other loose fill, organic types can be installed with little site preparation but need borders to contain them. In addition, be sure that you lay down dark-colored polyethylene film to prevent weeds from growing.	Bark, pine straw, and nutshells usually come in bags rather than in bulk, so they can be costly. Wood chips may be yours for the asking. Many towns give away chips from trees they have cleared.

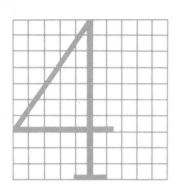

PLANNING
AND BUILDING
A PORCH

Successful outdoor living areas don't just happen. They require lots of thoughtful planning, attention to detail, and quality construction. Of the various outdoor living areas to choose from, a porch is one of the most difficult—but, ultimately, most rewarding—projects you're likely to take on. Essentially an addition, a porch has to harmonize with your home's appearance, connect comfortably to indoor living areas, and serve as a bridge to your yard. This chapter takes you step by step through the process of planning and building a new porch. Similarly, Chapter 5 shows you how to build other outdoor living areas.

SIZING UP THE SITUATION

Planning begins with a keen-eyed study of the house and lot. The object is simple: Determine what kind of porch will work best, and where. A number of factors, including those illustrated by the building project featured in this chapter, will affect your decisions.

Sometimes you can locate a porch at any of several different points, but that wasn't the case here. Setback requirements at the front of the house cut down on available space, and the side yards are relatively small. Building off the rear of the house (shown *at right* before the porch was added) was the most logical choice. Not only does this location offer enough room, but it also fits in best with this home's layout. Designed for relaxing and casual entertaining, a porch here would be handy to the home's kitchen. Of course, so was the existing brick patio. But it was exposed to the elements, and bringing out a tray of food or drinks entailed negotiating a door as well as several steps.

Often, a home's existing features influence a new porch's design. With this house, for instance, one problem was to avoid blocking rear windows on the first or second story.

Finally, you have to consider how you're going to get out to your new porch. Here the old back door would work just fine. At your house, you may need to cut a new doorway, or replace a window with a door.

GETTING A PLAN ON PAPER

No matter how good a porch looks in your mind's eye, building the one you want requires careful planning—on paper—through a series of meticulously developed drawings. Most architects and design consultants take each of the following

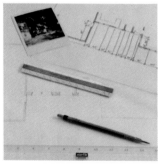

steps as they, and you, work toward the real thing.
• With photographs of the house and yard in hand, a professional begins by sketching a *rough drawing, top left,* of the existing floor plan. The drawing includes all pertinent dimensions as well as spatial relationships.
• The next step is to make a ¼-inch scale drawing of the rough floor plan. The *drafted drawing, above left,* must be accurate; later, the working drawings will be based, in part, on its dimensions and numerical relationships. At this point, too, a consultant makes

an *elevation drawing* (in essence, a head-on view or views), *above right,* of the existing structure.
• Now the porch itself enters the picture. Using tracing paper taped over the drafted drawings, a professional develops—in rough form—several possible design ideas for the addition *opposite above* and presents them to you, the client. At this point it's up to you to make suggestions, ask questions, and get satisfactory answers before agreeing to a particular plan.

• When everyone has settled on a basic design, the final step is to make this rough conception painstakingly precise. *Working drawings, opposite below,* which usually consist of individual floor plan, foundation, elevation, electrical, and construction detail drawings, do just that. Again, accuracy is pivotal: A contractor or subcontractors bid and build according to the specifications noted on the drawings.

To make a floor plan, for example, a consultant tapes tracing paper over the drafted drawing of the existing layout, pencils it in, and then begins the floor plan of the new porch, showing walls, doors,

windows, steps and landings, decking, and other elements. The plan is then "detailed" with *exact* dimensions and material specifications written directly on it. Detail drawings supply needed information not clearly spelled out in other places. Typically, an architect or design consultant includes details of the roof structure, roof framing, floor framing, and, often in the case of a porch, any landscaping changes.

(continued)

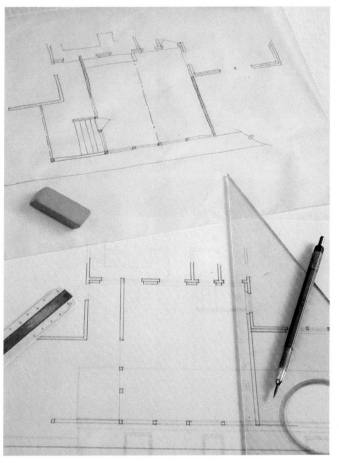

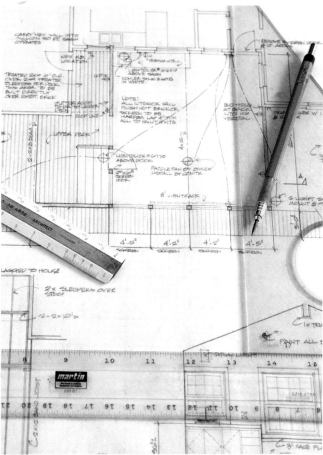

GETTING A PLAN ON PAPER

(continued)

At this stage, a professional consultant shares the working drawings with you to make sure you understand exactly what you're getting and, of course, to make sure you agree to it. Changes can still be made without trouble; minor ones probably will be noted right on the drawings.

If you're contracting the project yourself, now's the time to let the plan out for bids to various subcontractors. Always get at least three bids on all phases of construction. And before you decide on a particular subcontractor, ask for work references. Past customers are a subcontractor's best or worst advertisements. Also ask to see work that a subcontractor has performed.

With bids in hand, you're now ready to arrange financing. Most lenders will ask to see a set of the working drawings and may also want to check on the project during various stages of construction.

Once you've secured financing for the project, it's time to put your signature on the dotted line. You'll sign a contract with the general contractor—if there is one—or with the individual subcontractors you plan to use. Any contractor should also furnish a "Description of Materials" form, which lists the type and quality of building materials that will be used during construction.

Working drawings are the master plan. Subcontractors will bid based on the drawings' specifications.

The contract describes the terms of the agreement; the "Description of Materials" form details the type and quality of building materials.

GETTING OFF THE GROUND

Typically, construction begins with the excavation of the area. Regrading comes first, if necessary, followed by the digging of trenches for block or poured-concrete wall footings, or holes for posts if the project is a post-and-beam structure (which most porches are). Be sure to verify the location of all underground utilities before turning the first spade of earth.

For large-scale projects with concrete walls, you should call in a backhoe operator to dig the trenches for you. For post-and-beam projects, you can do the work yourself. In either case, the footings must be at or below the frost line to guard against heaving.

Framing the structure
Once the foundation is completed, framing can begin. In stud-wall construction, a wood sill plate caps the foundation walls. The floor joists go over the plate, followed by the floor decking, stud walls, ceiling joists, rafters and collar beams, and roof sheathing.

With post-and-beam construction—the method used to build the project featured in this chapter—posts rest atop pad footings. Beams fasten to the posts, and floor joists sit atop the beams. Or the joists are set flush with the top of the beams and are supported by hangers, as you can see by examining the framing details *at right*. Next come floor decking, stud walls, ceiling joists, rafters and collar beams, and roof sheathing.

1 A series of concrete pier footings, fortified with a length of ⅜-inch reinforcing rod, supports this addition. To guard against heaving, footings extend down to the frost line, which varies depending on the area of the country you live in. The tops of the footings rise several inches above grade to protect the posts from moisture in the ground.

2 The builder fastened a 2x12 support ledger at 2-foot intervals to the home's brick exterior wall, using long bolts that extend completely through the wall. You can do the same thing with lead anchors and lag screws. The ledger is set high enough to allow a smooth transition from the new addition to the house. A mason's line, stretched taut and fitted with a line level, helps ensure a level structure.

3 Pressure-treated 4x4 posts rest atop the footings. Reinforcing rods that protrude from the piers slip into ⅜-inch holes drilled into the bottoms of the posts, strengthening the whole structure by securing the posts to the footings. Doubled 2x12 beams are then toenailed to the top of the posts with galvanized nails.

4 Because the new porch is relatively large, a double 2x12 intercepter beam is positioned midway between the house and the porch's outer edge. Floor joists, supported by joist hangers, complete the support structure. Here, the tops of beams and joists are flush. Occasionally, floor joists are toenailed to the tops of beams, rather than set between them.

5 Vertical 2x6 plates fasten to the existing brick walls with lead anchors and lag screws. These plates facilitate attaching stud walls to the original structure by providing wood surfaces to nail to. Because it's easier to drill holes in mortar rather than in the bricks themselves, the anchors and lag screws are located at joints.

6 Underlayment-grade plywood decking covers the floor joists. In this instance, 2x6s spaced 24 inches on center and 2x6 top and sole plates make up the one stud wall. The other two walls are 6x6 posts and doubled 2x12 headers, as you can see in the photo *opposite*. Fiberboard sheathing is nailed to the stud wall.

FRAMING
THE ROOF

Putting a roof overhead comes next. Typically, post-and-beam construction features a large ridge beam that is "pocketed" into the existing house (the method used here) by removing masonry and inserting one end of the beam into the house wall. The other end of the beam is then set on a center, or ridge, post.

There are other common options. One is to *hang* a beam from the wall, rather than pocket it into position. This technique works especially well with frame houses and other structures where pocketing is difficult or impossible.

Another alternative (a different construction method altogether) makes use of prefabricated trusses, triangular assemblies that you simply nail atop the walls. With trusses, you don't need a ridge beam. Ordinarily, building with trusses is less expensive than post-and-beam framing and, if left exposed, gives an entirely different interior look.

Here 2x10s were selected for rafters to provide what architects call a good "interior reveal," meaning that they look more solid and more substantial than smaller framing members. In this case, the decision was entirely aesthetic. Building with 2x6s works equally well, bearing the weight of the load adequately and less expensively.

In this project, the rafters are nailed directly to the plate and ridge beam. Again, the choice was based on appearance; metal hangers would have done the same job just as effectively.

1 In this project, 6x6 posts support the roof and provide a stable, open framework for the two screened-in sides of the structure. Check the photo *opposite* and you can see how all but two posts were spaced 4 feet apart. (The narrower opening in the center will be a door.) Note in the photo *above* that the posts are notched on two sides to accept the 2x12 headers.

2 The headers are doubled to provide extra support for the heavy 2x10 rafters. Spacer blocks between the headers at their ends and at intervals along their lengths make each two-header unit into a member that is a full 5½ inches thick. A 2x6 plate on top of each pair of headers further ties them together and reinforces the structure.

3 The brick wall at the house end supports the roof's large ridge beam. The builder chiseled a pocket opening into the brick, then inserted the beam into it. On the other end, the beam rests atop a 6x6 support. The rafters, spaced 16 inches on center, were toenailed to the ridge beam and the walls' top plates. The ends of each rafter were cut at an angle determined by the roof's pitch.

4 Examine the plan drawing on page 67 and you'll notice that it calls for an asymmetric roof line, which means the rafters must terminate differently on one side than on the other. On the roof's long side, the builder made "bird's-mouth" cuts in the rafters so each can rest squarely on the top plate and still overhang the structure by several feet.

5 On the opposite, shorter side of the roof, the rafters were cut so their ends would be flush with the outer edge of the stud wall's top plate. As you can see by looking at this photo and photo number 4, a double plate was used atop each of the two walls that bear the rafters. A single 2x6 plate was sufficient on the other wall, because it carries no structural load.

6 The plan calls for an extended rake (gable overhang) at the end of the ridge beam. To create a soffit here, the builder made a framework of 2x4s for each side of the roof and secured them to the ridge beam and outer rafters. Finally, exterior drywall was nailed to the underside of each frame, sheathing the rakes.

CLOSING IN

The step-by-step photos *at right* depict the final stage in the construction process. When "closing in" is complete, only the finishing touches remain.

After weeks of planning and several more of enduring the bang-bang of building racket, most homeowners are understandably eager to move in and start enjoying the new surroundings as quickly as possible. However, resist the temptation until certain details are taken care of.

One detail is trim work; another is surface finishing—painting, usually—inside and out. As at other times during planning and building, the key to success is a slow and careful job.

Because construction work is a messy business, you'll have to completely clean the site. In some cases, areas of grass may even have to be resodded, the unhappy result of many major building projects.

Now, too, is an excellent time to consider landscaping changes. It's important to tie the porch not only to the house but to the yard, as well.

The photo *opposite* shows the beginning of a grade deck, which, as its name implies, is built flush with the existing grade line. An extension of a bigger patio deck next to the addition, the deck allows people to move easily from the above-grade porch to other spots in the yard.

1 With the framing complete, plywood roof sheathing was nailed to the rafters and covered with building felt. In this case, the sheathing was exterior siding, grooved every few inches along each panel. Applied face down, the siding looks, from the porch's interior, like individual board decking (see the photo on pages 76 and 77). Note that a post has been installed to support the extended eave.

2 To trim out the roof, a redwood fascia board—finger-jointed at the peak—was nailed to the eave and rake edges. A metal drip edge will also be nailed to the eaves and rake so water will properly drain off the roof. At the house end of the roof (not shown), flashing seals the joint where house and porch meet. Now shingling can begin.

3 An intermediate-level deck—two steps below the porch floor and one step above the grade-level deck—was constructed at this point. This deck was made from a framework of 2x8s attached to the posts of the porch and to the house. Then decking boards were attached to the joists. Note that sheathing and siding have been applied to the walls, and trim work has been started.

4 To bridge the difference in grade between the floor of the porch and the mid-level deck, stairs were constructed and secured with nails and bolts. Plywood behind the stairs conceals the insulation board on the edge of the porch and more will be added to cover the short wall at the end of the stairs. The stairs' risers will later be closed in with siding.

5 Removable panels, fitted between the support posts, provide access to hideaway storage beneath the porch. The panels consist of 2x4 frames, covered with plywood and siding. Polyethylene film laid on the earth under the porch acts as a vapor barrier to keep the crawl space clean and dry, creating a handy place to stash lawn furniture and barbecue gear during the winter.

6 To fashion the grade-level deck, a 4-inch bed of sand was spread over the entire excavated area, followed by a layer of polyethylene film that serves as a vapor barrier. Then treated fir 2x4s were laid flat, and 2x6 decking was nailed to them, as shown *opposite*. Another tread/riser assembly ties the porch to the deck. At this point, all that remains is painting and the other finishing touches discussed at left.

MOVING IN

Here, at last, is the end result of the porch project you've seen taking shape on the preceding pages. With screens and a door in place, a ceiling fan installed to aid circulation, and the new space furnished in breezy rattan, the owners have gained what amounts to an outdoor living room.

The addition measures approximately 16x22 feet, and its cathedral ceiling and exposed, oversize rafters *at left* make it feel even more spacious. Light colors and rattan furniture visually expand the space, too.

The dining area in the foreground of our photo is only a few steps from the kitchen—and equally convenient to the intermediate and grade-level decks *below*. Food barbecued out here can go directly to the table for bug-free dining.

The decks also provide a smooth transition from the porch to the yard and woods beyond. What started out, then, as one project actually results in three outdoor living areas—the screened porch, a shady intermediate-level deck, and a sunny patio deck.

Even though this contemporary porch abuts a traditional brick home, the materials used—roof shingles, siding, and other exterior features—successfully tie together old and new. Too many porches look like tacked-on afterthoughts. This one adds architectural distinction, along with well-planned outdoor living spaces. The months of planning, decision-making, and noisy construction work are well worth the effort when a porch as nice as this one is finally ready to enjoy.

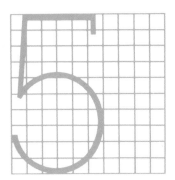

BUILDING OTHER OUTDOOR LIVING AREAS

The previous chapter explains how to build a porch—the most ambitious yard project likely to happen at any house. This chapter takes you through some less complex ventures. By adding a deck or patio, you create a second living room in natural surroundings. With a fence or wall, you define borders and create privacy. And carefully placed retaining walls tame sloping property and help shape unexpected seating or activity areas. Best of all, most of these amenities are well within the range of most do-it-yourselfers' abilities.

PATIOS

Before you begin to plan your patio, be sure to check all lot restrictions, including zoning regulations, building codes, the locations of underground utilities, and any limitations contained in your property deed. Then, determine the size and shape of your patio. If a rectangle won't work, plan other geometric shapes or free-form curves. Add borders, or divide the design into smaller sections.

Concrete is one of the most popular and durable patio surfaces. In the box *opposite*, step-by-step instructions show how to pour it. Illustrated *below* are four popular textured finishes for concrete.

The *swirl*, perhaps the easiest to achieve, results from working a magnesium or steel trowel or a wood float over a screeded slab in an arclike fashion. The tool you use will determine how coarse the finish will be. All the finishing tools produce at least a slightly rough, slip-resistant surface.

For a *broomed* surface, pull a push broom across a slab of just-troweled concrete. The degree of texture you get depends on how stiff the broom bristles are. Take the broomed look a step further by creating a *checkerboard* pattern. Borders make this one especially effective.

For an *exposed aggregate* finish, sprinkle aggregate over a screeded concrete surface, and work it into the concrete with a float. An hour after embedding the stones, spray a fine mist over the surface and scrub it—but not too hard— with a broom. Keep scrubbing until you can see the tops of the pebbles. (For more about concrete, see pages 48-51.)

(continued)

TEXTURING CONCRETE

SWIRL

BROOMED

CHECKERBOARD

EXPOSED AGGREGATE

POURING A CONCRETE PATIO

1 Stake out the shape, allowing room for the forms that will hold the concrete. Outline the site's perimeter with string, pour sand over the string to transfer the perimeter line to the ground, then remove the string and excavate the site. The slab should be 2 to 4 inches thick, rest on 2 inches of sand or gravel, and rise above the grade by approximately 1 inch.

2 Build forms using 2x4s for the straight runs, and locating support stakes every 3 to 4 feet. For curves, use ¼-inch exterior plywood or hardboard, spacing stakes every 1 to 2 feet. Brace the forms with 1x4 stakes wherever two forms meet, as shown here.

3 Lay reinforcing wire mesh into the form, keeping the wire edges an inch or two from the edge of the forms. For slabs wider than 5 feet—the width of the wire mesh—overlap sections by one square of mesh, and join the pieces with wire. Flatten the mesh by walking on it.

4 Begin placing the concrete in the least accessible part of your site, building a bridge, as shown, if you're using a wheelbarrow to pour the concrete. As you pour, tamp the concrete to fill any air pockets, especially in the corners and along the perimeter. While pouring, use a claw hammer or rake to pull the wire mesh into the center of the slab's thickness.

5 Begin screeding as soon as you've filled the first few feet of the form. With the aid of a helper, move the 2x4 screed back and forth in a sawing motion, keeping both ends of the screed on the top edges of opposing forms, as shown. Fill any low spots with additional concrete if necessary.

6 After screeding, use a darby or bull float to further smooth the surface and to embed the stones in the concrete below. Then wait until the water sheen disappears from the slab's surface before applying the desired finish.

LAYING A BRICK PATIO

1 Outline the perimeter with stakes and string. Pour sand over the string to transfer the line to the ground. Then, make room for a border, remove the string, and dig out a shallow channel to define your patio's perimeter. Remove enough sod and soil from the entire site so that the paving material can rest 1 inch above the grade on a 2-inch bed of fill sand.

2 Before proceeding further, check the site to make sure that water drains away from any structure adjoining it. (The slope should be at least ¼ inch per foot.) To stop plants from growing between the bricks, spray weed killer over the ground, and cover the area with overlapping sheets of dark, 4-mil polyethylene film as shown.

3 Fill the border channel with a small amount of sand, then position bricks, lumber, or other materials for a border. Tap the bricks with the handle of a trowel or hammer, packing sand around the bricks as you work. Next, spread a 2-inch bed of well-compacted sand inside the border. Using a 2x4 with the ends notched to fit over the edging, screed the sand until it's level.

4 Starting in a corner, lay the patio bricks on the bed of sand, again tapping the bricks into place. Try one of the patterns shown *opposite, below,* or a design of your own creation. In either case, don't disturb the sand as you work, and make sure the bricks are equally spaced.

Next to concrete, brick is probably the most popular patio material. And laying bricks in sand is even easier than pouring concrete. You'll also find that bricks are available in a range of earth tones, shapes, and sizes, and can be laid in a variety of patterns, as shown *opposite, below.*

The first thing to do after choosing a site is to determine how many bricks to buy. A little simple arithmetic will provide the answer. First multiply the length of the patio by the width to get the area in square feet. Add 10 percent of this number to allow for waste. Then multiply the total square footage by 5.2 (the number of patio bricks and joints between them covering 1 square foot).

Plan on using a lot of sand, which commonly is sold by the ton. Assuming you're going to lay patio bricks with a 2-inch base of sand beneath them, first figure the area's size in cubic feet by multiplying length times width times depth. Then

let your dealer convert this number into the amount of sand necessary to do the job. If you plan to fill the joints between bricks with sand, add an extra ton of sand for every 800 bricks.

Once you have the materials on hand, lay a sample section to see how it looks. Leave a ⅛- to ¼-inch space between the bricks.

As a final step in planning, consider laying a border around your patio. Place bricks vertically, diagonally, or any other way that's both attractive and functional.

Alternatives to patio bricks are other masonry materials such as concrete patio blocks or flat stones (slate or flagstone, for example). These also can be laid in sand. To learn what's available in your area, visit a local brickyard, home center, or building stone supplier. (For more information about paving materials, see pages 48-51.)

PLANNING AND BUILDING A PORCH

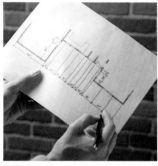

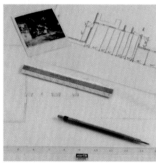

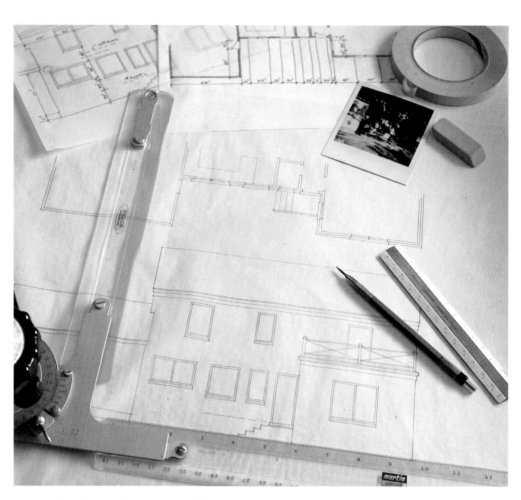

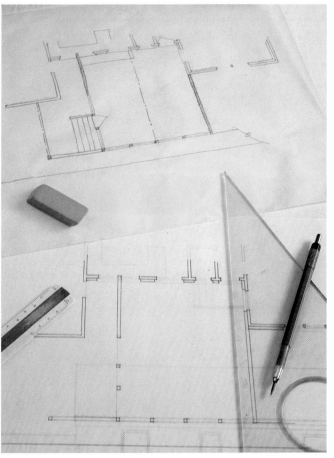

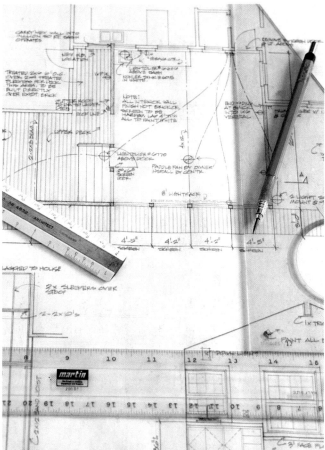

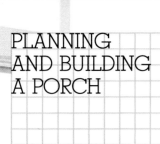

PLANNING AND BUILDING A PORCH

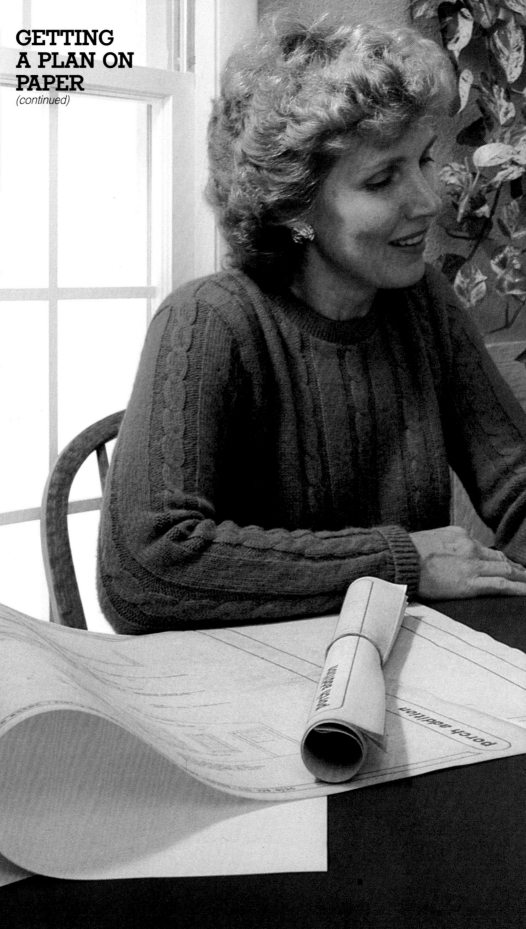

PLANNING AND BUILDING A PORCH

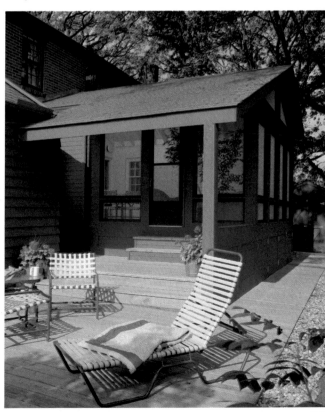

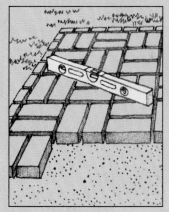

5 To make sure that bricks are aligned properly, stretch a mason's line between the border's opposite edges. Place the line where you expect the outer edge of your next course of bricks to be. Then lay the bricks to the line, tapping them down or adding sand beneath them as necessary. Periodically, check for level or proper slope.

7 When all the bricks are set in place, spread a thin layer of damp sand over the surface. Let it dry for several hours, then brush the sand into the joints. Brush gently at first so you don't dislodge the bricks. To hold the bricks even more tightly together, use dry mortar mix instead of sand.

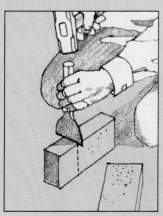

6 To trim a brick to size, first mark it with a cutoff line. Then place the brick on sand or loose soil. Place a brick set on the line, and tap the set with a sledge, using enough force to score the break point. Make the final cut by holding the brick set perpendicular to the brick's surface, with the bevel facing the waste side. Now, strike the brick set sharply. The brick should split apart.

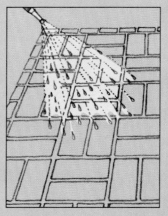

8 Once the cracks are full, wet the entire area with a fine spray of water. The moisture will help the sand or mortar mix settle between the joints and will also wash away any remaining particles from the surface. You'll probably have to brush in additional material and spray several times more before the joints are completely packed. When they are packed, let the surface dry and sweep it clean.

PATIO BRICK PATTERNS

BASKET WEAVE

DIAGONAL HERRINGBONE

HERRINGBONE

RUNNING

DECKS

Many people shy away from building a deck because they fear that the work is beyond their abilities. In most cases, they're wrong. But before picking up hammer and saw, you *do* have to understand what a deck is, how it's framed, what size materials you need, and how you put them all together. Let this and the following pages be your guide.

WHERE TO BUILD

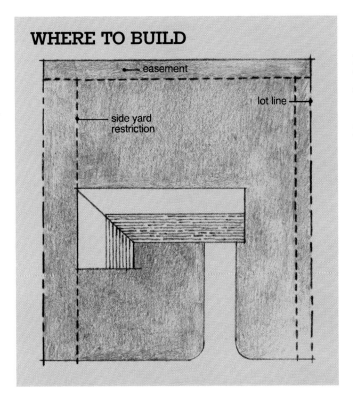

P lan carefully. The size and style of a deck depend largely on how you intend to use it—for outdoor entertaining, cooking, or just sitting.

Where you build a deck and how high you plan to make it also depend on the needs that the deck will serve and your home's relation to its site (see illustration, *opposite*).

Finally, before selecting a location, consider possible lot restrictions, such as those shown in the example *at left*. A zoning regulation or easement could require you to build several feet in from your property line. Building codes may also affect your plans, as may the locations of service lines; contact local utilities to find out where your lines are located.

CONSTRUCTION BASICS

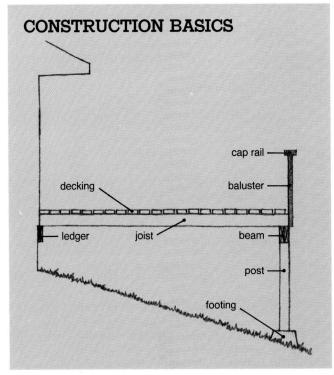

T here's no mystery to a deck's post-and-beam construction, *left*. The *decking* rests on *joists* and *beams*, which gain support from *posts* or masonry piers on belowground *footings*. And, unless it's freestanding, a deck is tied to the house structure by a *ledger*. In some cases, joists rest on top of the ledger; in others, they butt against the ledger and are held in place by metal fasteners. On some decks, the posts extend up through the decking to function as part of the railing. On others, *balusters* fasten to joists or beams. A *cap rail* stabilizes and protects the other railing members.

DECK ALTERNATIVES

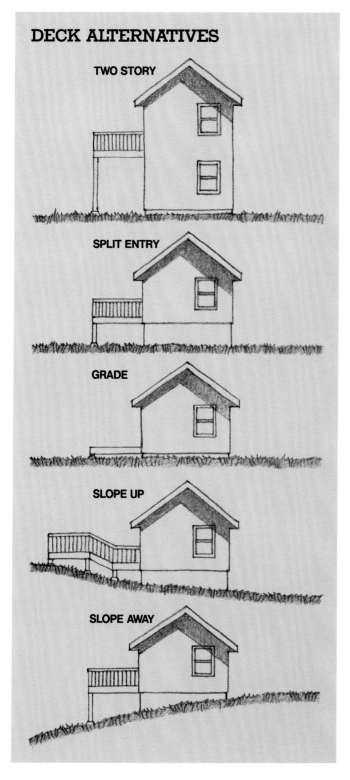

TWO STORY

SPLIT ENTRY

GRADE

SLOPE UP

SLOPE AWAY

BEAM AND JOIST SPAN TABLE

Beam Size	Maximum Distance Between Posts		
4x6	6 ft.		
4x8	8 ft.		
4x10	10 ft.		
4x12	12 ft.		

	Span at Different Spacings		
Joist Size	16 in.	24 in.	32 in.
2x6	8 ft.	6 ft.	5 ft.
2x8	10 ft.	8 ft.	7 ft.
2x10	13 ft.	10 ft.	8 ft.

When you're planning to buy materials, you need to know what size members will work best. The span chart *above* notes a wide range of possibilities that allow you to correctly space posts and joists, depending on beam and joist sizes. Keep in mind, too, that when post lengths exceed 8 feet, you'll need to switch from 4x4s to 6x6s for extra strength.

Use only redwood, cedar, or pressure-treated wood for framing members. All structural parts of a deck should be resistant to rot.

How does it fit?

How you situate a deck depends on the style of your house and the topography of your property. Some designs fit certain homes better than others, as shown in the illustration *at left*.

For a two-story or split-entry home, tall supporting posts make it possible to extend the deck from an upstairs room. For a ranch-style home, an on-grade deck lifts you off the ground, but not high enough to require railings. For a house with ground sloping up behind it, consider building a free-standing deck, attached with stairs and a landing. And, if the ground slopes away, reach out with an elevated deck.

Regardless of style, deck surfaces are usually constructed at least 1½ inches lower than the interior floor they serve. This promotes good drainage and also allows for easy access to the deck.

Avoid an awkward "added-on" look by blending your deck with the design and color of your home. Paint or stain the deck the same color as other exterior woodwork, or, if your deck is constructed from garden-grade redwood or cedar, allow it to weather to a natural, unstained color.

(continued)

SETTING POSTS

1 With your plan on paper, gather a tape measure and several 1x2 stakes, and begin staking out the site. Mark the intended location of the ledger on the house (if the deck is not freestanding), then build *batter boards* at the corners and run a mason's line around the site's perimeter. Check that the corners are square, either by measuring the diagonals between opposite corners, or by using the 3-4-5 method as shown and explained on page 88.

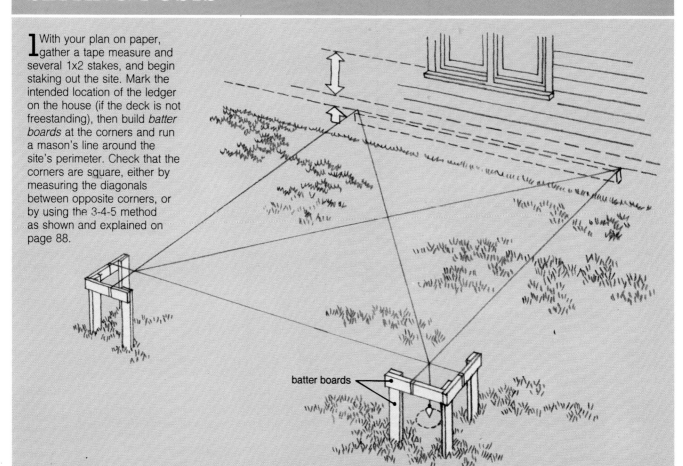

batter boards

2 If you're using a pair of 2x10s or other members of comparable strength to make a beam, space 4x4 support posts every 8 to 10 feet. These should rest on or in a concrete pier or footing to prevent rot and to guard against movement of any kind. For the posts, dig 8-inch-wide postholes that extend below the frost line. Use either a manually operated post-hole digger or a power-driven auger.

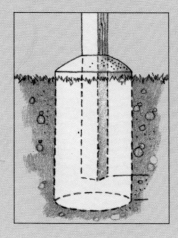

3 If you're using concrete, first pour it into the holes. Unless the project is unusually large, you should be able to get by using pre-mixed concrete in bags, rather than ordering the ready-mixed kind. When making footings, raise the concrete at least 2 inches above grade, and taper it around the post so it sheds water. (If you're using metal post anchors, you should install these now.)

CONSTRUCTION TIPS

1 While the concrete is still fresh, set 4x4 posts into it, as shown in the drawing here. Attach outrigger stakes to steady the post until the concrete sets. Using a level, plumb the post on two sides, checking your readings twice. Also, make sure the posts you erect are in perfect alignment with one another.

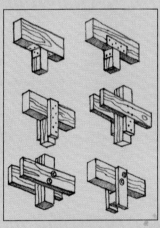

2 Using one of the methods shown here, secure the beams to the posts. To run the posts up through the decking as supports for the deck's railing, fashion the beams from two lengths of 1½-inch-thick lumber, and sandwich the posts between them. For an on-grade deck you won't need a railing; cut the posts to the correct height and fasten the beams atop them. Anchor the beams with bolts or large wood screws.

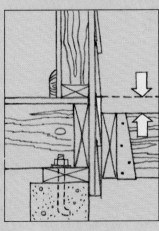

3 Before attaching a ledger strip—usually a 2x8 or 2x10—to the side of the house, decide whether you want the joists to rest atop the ledger or abut it with joist hangers, as shown here. Then, using lag screws, attach the ledger to the house framing. If the house has lap siding, invert a piece for a shim. To fasten ledgers to a solid concrete or concrete block foundation, use lag screws and expansion anchors.

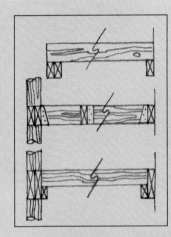

4 Selecting the right size of joist depends on the spans involved (see the chart on page 83); 2x6s, 2x8s, and 2x10s are most common. Fasten joists to the ledger at the house end and to a beam between posts at the other. Use either joist hangers or cleats. Maintain 16-inch intervals between joists, and secure the members in place with galvanized nails. (The non-galvanized types will stain the finish.)

5 Deck material typically consists of 2x4s, but 2x2s or 2x6s also work well. Lay them perpendicular to the joists, using a ¼-inch spacer strip. Or, if you like, install them in a diagonal pattern. Before nailing deck boards, check the end grain to make sure the tree rings hump upward. Then drive a pair of galvanized nails into the boards at each joist location.

6 After you've nailed the decking in place, go back and snap a chalk line along the edges. Set up a straightedge the appropriate distance from the chalk line, adjust the blade on a circular saw to just below the thickness of the decking, then trim off the irregular board ends. Allow a generous slack with the electrical cord so it doesn't hinder your cutting.

STAIRS AND RAILINGS

If your deck is elevated at any point, you'll probably need to add either stairs or a railing, or both. The National Building Code, which many local building inspectors adhere to, requires a step or steps for outdoor access to any deck rising 8 inches or more above grade. If the deck is 30 inches or more above grade, then a railing is also necessary. Don't be put off by the prospect of building stairs or railings. Use the advice on this and the following page to guide your work. The result will be a deck that's not only up to code, but, more important, a place that's safe for you and your family.

BUILDING STAIRS

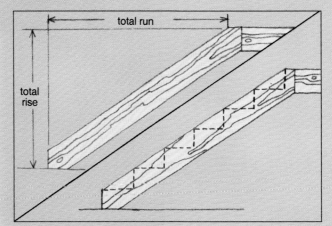

1 First measure the total rise and run, as illustrated here. A typical step has a 6¼- to 8¼-inch rise (including the thickness of the tread—usually 1½ inches) and a 9¾- to 12¾-inch tread. Divide combinations of these figures into the total rise and run, respectively, until you get the same whole number. This is the number of steps you'll need.

2 Next, mark the lengths of treads and risers on a framing square, as shown. Position the square so its edges and the 2x10 or 2x12 stringer meet at the marks. Pencil in the correct proportions for each step. The height of the bottom step is less than the others; subtract the tread thickness from the bottom riser.

3 Cut out the first stringer and use it as a pattern for the second. After both are cut, use metal hangers or bolts to secure them to the deck's perimeter. Nail the treads to the stringers, allowing them to either overlap or remain flush with their sides. Anchor the base of the steps to a concrete footing, using drift pins, expansion anchors, or angle irons.

BUILDING RAILINGS

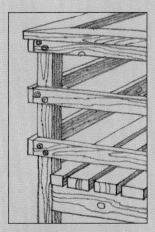

For safety, stairways or elevated decks need railings. The National Building Code specifies that a railing be at least 3 feet high, with no more than 6 inches between horizontal rails or between balusters and other vertical members. This drawing shows how a post extends above the deck to serve as a support for the railing. The horizontals are 2x4s nailed or screwed to the posts. A 2x6 cap protects the top from moisture.

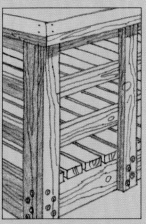

This strong railing system is made of 2x4 vertical posts secured with lag screws to the beam and joists. Note how the posts are doubled in the corner, where extra strength is required. One-inch boards serve as intermediate rails; a 2x4, mitered at the corner, caps the railing. This railing could easily be adapted to a stairway; for extra strength there, attach posts to the stringers with lag bolts, not lag screws.

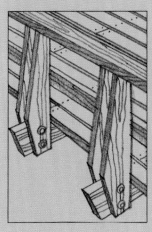

Still another option is the double-post system shown here. In this arrangement, posts are cut from 2-inch stock, bolted to both sides of extended joists, and then rails are attached to the posts. Inserted into pre-drilled holes, two bolts for each vertical tightly hold everything together. Joist ends cut at an angle create design interest.

RAILING STYLES

A deck railing must be strong and safe, but don't feel you're limited to the styles shown *at left*. Look over the selection shown *below*, or create a design of your own that·is both stylish and functional.

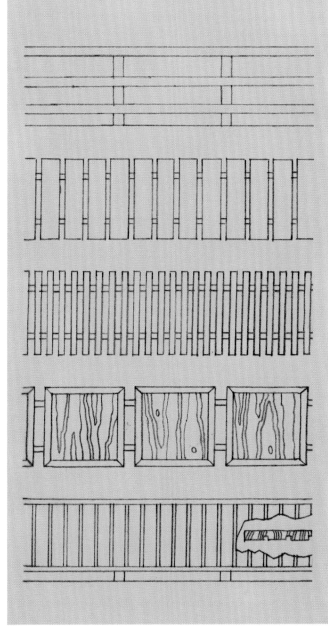

FENCES AND GATES

Just as the reasons for building a fence vary, so, too, do fence styles and materials—from vinyl-coated or galvanized metal fences, to more expensive wood varieties made of cedar or pressure-treated lumber. Regardless of the style and material you choose, most fences are laid out and constructed in the way shown here. For more about fence styles, turn to page 90. And to learn how to hang a gate in your new fence, see page 91.

BUILDING A FENCE

1 Before you begin the work, check with local building officials to find out if any codes will affect your project and whether or not you need a permit. Next, determine exactly where your property lines are and contact utility companies to find out the locations of any buried service lines. After you select a site for the fence, locate the terminal posts (ends and corners) and gate posts, and mark them with stakes.

2 Use line to connect the corner and end posts, then check them for square with the 3-4-5 method shown here: Measure 3 feet along one side, 4 feet along the other; the distance between these two points should be 5 feet. If a corner is not 90 degrees, figure the angle on graph paper, cut a plywood scrap to fit, and use it as a guide.

3 Dig postholes 24 to 30 inches into the ground. If you are digging just a few holes, you can get by using a manually operated clamshell digger or auger. Augers work best in rock-free soil. But if you have a lot of holes to dig, or lots of rocks to contend with, rent a power-driven auger, like the one shown on page 84.

4 Cedar, redwood, and pressure-treated lumber resist rot for years, but other kinds of wood are not as hardy. Protect these other kinds by using a preservative such as creosote, pentachlorophenol (or penta), or copper naphthenate. Apply with a brush, or soak the wood in the preservative itself, paying special attention to post tops and areas where you've made cuts. Later, paint the post with a good exterior paint or stain.

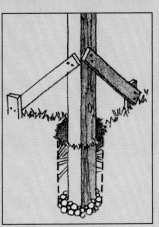

5 To set the first post, pour a few inches of gravel into the hole. Stand a post in the hole, and plumb it in two directions, bracing with outriggers, as shown here. Pour in a little more gravel around the base of the post, then fill the remainder of the cavity with premixed concrete. Use a pipe to tamp the concrete and remove any air pockets.

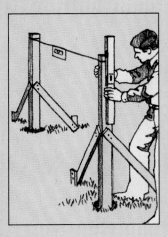

6 Following the procedure described in Step 5, plumb and set the other end and corner posts. To ensure that they're all equal in height, stretch a line between them, and hang a line level midway along the line. Once the posts are level, add the concrete.

7 Gate posts also should be set in concrete, but before adding the material, check the gate opening for square. Measure both diagonals and the distance between posts at top and bottom, as shown. Equal top and bottom measurements and equal diagonals indicate a square opening. Install the intermediate posts, using the leveled lines as a guide. Pour gravel around the base of these posts, and fill the remaining cavity with compacted earth.

8 After the posts are set, cut rails and screening, then coat all components with a good exterior paint or stain. Once the finish is dry, fasten the rails to the posts, using one of the joinery techniques shown here and securing the rails with galvanized nails, screws, or bolts. As you work, keep the rails level and at least 6 inches above the ground.

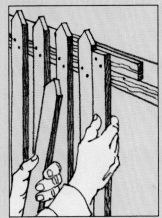

9 The last step is to add the screening. If you choose pickets, slats, or boards, cut a spacer to the desired width, and nail a cleat to one end, as shown. Hang the spacer on the top rail, and work off the preceding screening member. Occasionally check with a level to make sure that the screening is plumb.

FENCES AND GATES

(continued)

How you want a fence to work—plus how you want it to look—will go a long way toward determining the style you choose.

Even if you already have a good idea of what style of fence to build, take a trip around the neighborhood and observe how other people have handled similar situations. At the same time, check out home improvement books and magazines for suggestions, any of which you can either duplicate or alter to satisfy your own taste. Also, ask employees of a lumberyard or home center for tips on types that work and look best for various kinds of lots.

Finally, study the typical styles illustrated *at right.* Many are available in prefab form, which saves you time-consuming cutting and fitting.

Wind warnings

Fences are designed to keep out stray animals and other wandering objects, but not every fence will keep unruly winds from playing havoc with your yard. In fact, a solid fence may even increase the problem: Wind currents tend to "leap" over a solid fence, causing a vacuum on the wind-sheltered side, and pulling the air down again.

If you live in a locale with strong prevailing winds, you can slow them down with openwork screening: Slats, latticework, and bamboo are three effective options. Louvers are doubly worthwhile because they not only lower the wind's velocity but also redirect the currents.

FENCE STYLES

BUILDING A GATE

A fence must weather wind, rain, and snow, but otherwise it just stands there. A gate, too, has to withstand weather's worst, and it also must be sturdy enough to take the same kind of wear and tear that any front door endures. What's more, because it's often a highly visible part of your home's landscaping scheme, a gate should call attention to itself, yet harmonize with the adjoining fence or wall.

Gate designs vary even more widely than fence styles. Some are simply barn-type half doors that continue the lines of the fence. Other designs are delicate, decorative openwork that are arched or curved and are sometimes sheltered by rose-covered arbors.

For best results, hang a gate before attaching screening, so you can correct an out-of-square opening. Use sturdy fasteners and rustproof hardware.

1 The illustration *at left* shows a finished gate already installed. Typically, gates are at least 3 feet wide and must hang level and square between the posts. Depending on the gate's thickness, the space between gate posts and the sides of the gate will range between ¼ and ½ inch. Clearance below should be at least an inch, more if the gate will swing over upward sloping land or vegetation.

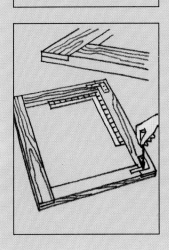

2 Cut the wood members of the gate frame to size and assemble them. Use butt, lapped, or half-lapped joints at the corners of the frame. To strengthen the corners, bond the joints with waterproof building adhesive and secure metal angle plates to them. Most important, square the corners, as shown here.

3 Brace the frame with a diagonal piece of wood running from the hinge side to the latch side. Toenail it in place with galvanized nails. Cut the screening members to measure and add them one by one. Or nail on random lengths and trim around the perimeter of the gate with a portable circular saw.

4 Drill pilot holes where the hinges will be, then screw or bolt the hinges to the gate. Use scrap wood to prop the gate in the opening, and screw or bolt the gate to the post. Keep in mind that most gates swing inward, and, because many are also fairly heavy, three equally spaced hinges are necessary for adequate support.

5 Add latches to the top or side of the gate. Of the three types shown, two can be attached easily with screws. However, the thumb latch *at left, top,* requires boring to install. With the latch in place, close the gate and mark its inside edge on the latch post. The last step is to nail on a strip of wood here to serve as a stop.

RETAINING WALLS

Few outdoor structures work as hard as a retaining wall. Made from natural stone, concrete, or other lasting materials, a retaining wall provides a reliable way to tame an unruly bank or slope, stop damaging erosion, and add visual appeal to a landscape. The skills required to build a retaining wall are relatively simple, but the work itself is difficult and repetitive. If you plan to use large stones, you may want to have an assistant help with the heavy lifting.

RETAINING WALL OPTIONS

Are you looking for a unique way to terrace a portion of your yard? Try placing railroad ties on end, as shown *at left*. Dig a trench from one-third to one-half the length of the ties. (For short walls, cut ties to the desired height above grade, plus the depth of the trench.) Then set the ties in the trench, and pack dirt around them.

Pressure-treated lumber also makes an attractive, fence-like retaining wall. For the one shown *at left*, 4x4 posts were sunk into the ground, then 2x8s were fastened to the posts with lag screws. Again, one-third to one-half of the posts' lengths should be below ground.

In the drawing *at left*, a block retaining wall frames a graduated deck and patio. Steps set into the wall lead to the high ground beyond. Capping the block wall is a single course of bricks (called *coping*), which, aside from being attractive, prevents rain from filling the blocks' hollow cores.

BUILDING A RUBBLESTONE RETAINING WALL

1 Before beginning, consult with building authorities. Local codes may determine how you can and can't proceed. Then stake and lay out the wall's front perimeter. Remove the sod, and dig a trench 6 to 12 inches deep, slightly wider than the wall.

2 Provide for drainage by filling the trench to just below grade with pea gravel or small rocks. Next, set large stones on the gravel base. Ideally, these first stones should span the base. Use successively smaller stones for the upper courses.

3 For the second and higher courses, stagger joints for greater strength. Prevent wobbling by filling gaps and low spots with small pieces of stone or troweled-in soil. As you work, be sure to tilt the stones toward the embankment. If you need to cut stones to fit, use a mason's hammer and brick set.

4 To finish the wall, spread a 2-inch-thick mortar bed over the next-to-last course. Press in large, flat stones, filling the gaps with smaller ones. When you're lifting heavy stones, let your legs—not your back—do most of the work. And don't be shy about asking someone to help move extra-large stones.

OTHER WALL FAVORITES

Ashlar stone is cut on four sides, so it's fairly easy to stack. You'll still have to do some final cutting and matching, though.

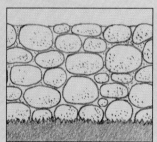

Fieldstone held together with mortar must be cut and fitted. You can apply the mortar more liberally than if you were using brick or block.

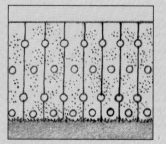

Poured concrete walls require forms, which you build or rent. These sturdy walls have footings and are reinforced with rods.

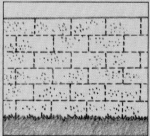

Hurry your wall-building along by dry-laying blocks, then bonding them with fiberglass-reinforced mortar applied to the surface.

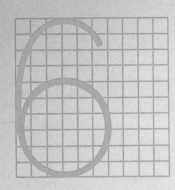

6

OUTFITTING YOUR YARD

Like the interior of your home, your yard needs proper furnishings and equipment. The right tools help you groom and maintain plants, trees, and grasses. Furniture and outdoor cookers promote gracious outdoor living. Watering systems keep your lawn lush and green. Lighting adds drama, safety, and security—and extends the hours you can enjoy the great outdoors. This chapter presents a sampling of yard amenities you can buy, along with guidelines about what to look for when you shop.

PORTABLE SUNSHADES

Bright sunshine may tempt you outdoors, but too much will quickly send you back inside. Outdoor shading should be part of your landscape plan. If your yard lacks natural shade or permanent structures such as arbors, trellises, or gazebos, consider portable solutions.

Of these, the most familiar shade device is the old-fashioned canvas umbrella. The updated pyramid-shape version shown here opens manually, and its wooden pole can be set into a table or secured in its own base. When clustered, several umbrellas create a mobile outdoor room.

The scalloped umbrella in the center of the photo is made of vinyl, with a metal frame and pole. A crank and chain, which attach to the hardware on the pole, make it easy to open and close.

Portable shade also can come in a less familiar package. The freestanding circular sunshade shown here is made of polymer canvas, a material that doesn't change color or buckle with prolonged exposure to heat and light. Vinyl strips hold the canvas taut in its frame. Everything about this model is adjustable—from the position of the entire unit and the height of the pole to the circular canvas, which moves in an arc so you can stay in the shade as the angle of the sun changes.

95

OUTFITTING YOUR YARD TOOLS

Our photo shows just a sampling of the almost limitless selection of tools available today—but you don't necessarily need a lot of gear to keep your yard in shape. Start with a rake or two, a hoe, a shovel, a spade, shears, a trowel, a mower, and a good pair of work gloves. Then, depending on your landscaping and inclinations, add more specialized items such as a power weed trimmer, a leaf blower, and pruning saws. Most important, whether you're buying simple hand tools or sophisticated power models, shop for quality materials and construction.

With hand tools, quality and price are based on considerations such as construction and the gauge of steel. The fewer welded parts there are the better, because welds are apt to break with time. Look for ash or hickory wood handles; they provide a more comfortable grip than plastic or steel and are less likely to snap than other woods.

Power tools can help you do many jobs faster. Battery-operated equipment is suited to small jobs and light use; conventional electric tools are popular and efficient, but their use is limited by the length of your extension cord. Gas-powered machinery offers more power and mobility, but is also much noisier.

Maintain your tools by brushing off dirt, grass clippings, and other debris after each use. Clean more thoroughly as needed. Prevent rust on steel by occasionally wiping it with petroleum oil; linseed oil protects wooden handles.

Power tools deserve annual tune-ups; sharpen any cutting edge, whether on a power or hand tool, at the beginning of the gardening season.

Store tools in a clean, dry place—one that's easily accessible to you but out of the reach of small children.

FURNITURE

Outdoor furniture has come a long way since the days of flimsy aluminum chairs with saggy canvas or scratchy plastic-strip seats. Today, most furniture designed for outdoor use is durable enough to be enjoyed for many years, attractive enough to use almost anywhere, and—as our photo demonstrates—available in a wide range of styles and materials. Here's how they compare.

When you're shopping for outdoor furniture, consider comfort, mobility, upkeep, and weather resistance.

• *Comfort.* Wood, plastic, aluminum, steel, wrought iron, wicker, rattan—just about any material can provide the framework for comfortable outdoor seating. The key is to select sturdy pieces that fit *your* frame. In the store, stretch out on lounge chairs, sit at tables, and bounce up and down a bit on the chairs.

• *Mobility.* Heavy iron and wood pieces all but root themselves in place; wicker, rattan, plastic, and aluminum are more easily moved to take advantage of sun or shade. Folding and stacking furniture offers the ultimate in mobility and takes up minimum storage space.

• *Upkeep.* Scratch- and corrosion-resistant finishes on tubular-steel, aluminum, or molded-plastic frames guarantee long life and low maintenance. Fabrics for seating and upholstery include synthetics, vinyls, and canvases—all treated to resist dirt, water, mildew, and fading. Many can be cleaned with soap and water. Redwood, teak, and pressure-treated lumber can be stained or allowed to weather naturally; protect other wood furniture with a durable finish. Enameled wrought iron holds up well outdoors, but scratches may require periodic touch-ups to prevent rust.

• *Weather resistance.* Any material that spends its life outdoors is bound to weather to a certain extent, but some materials stand up to sun and moisture better than others. Wicker, rattan, and canvas, for example, make sense only for a covered porch or patio, where they're not exposed directly to the elements.

99

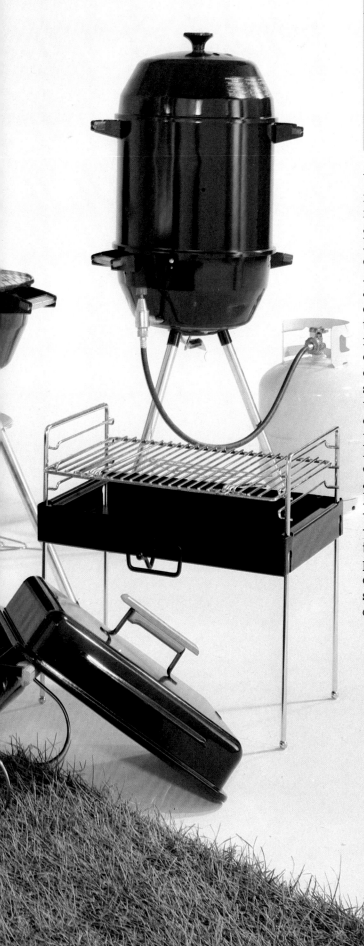

Whether it's hot dogs or fresh-caught salmon, food prepared outdoors always seems to taste better. In fact, outdoor cookers are among America's hottest-selling appliances and, as you can see on these pages, there's a lot to choose from. Do you prefer to cook on smokers or grills? Which fuel source do you want to use—charcoal, gas, or electricity? Should your unit be freestanding, built-in, a roll-around, or one you can carry along on trips to the lake? What's the best way to get a meal on your family's picnic table? Whatever your preference is, an outdoor cooking unit is sure to bring you hours of eating enjoyment.

Cooking over charcoal first hit America in the early 1950s and soon nearly every backyard became an outdoor kitchen. Small wonder: Food seared by the intense heat of a charcoal fire tastes great, and you keep the mess of cooking outdoors.

Relatively inexpensive, charcoal grills range from tabletop hibachis and fold-up picnic units to large braziers, kettles, and wagons. Cast-iron models last longer than steel units, but are heavy to move. The main drawbacks of charcoal cooking are the time required to light and heat the briquettes and the messy cleanup.

• *Gas grills* are easy to start and clean to cook on, and their heat can be finely regulated. The key to how a gas grill works lies with its permanent ceramic briquettes. Fired by natural or LP gas burners, these porous rocks catch meat juices, then flare up just as charcoal does. It's this action—not the smell of charcoal itself—that gives grilled food its unique taste. Permanently mounted grills require a natural-gas hookup; portable grills use bottled gas.

• *Electric grills* also include ceramic briquettes. Electric units are portable (as far as the cord reaches) and are easy to use and clean—but temperature is harder to regulate than with gas grills.

• *Smokers* use a combination of heat, moisture, and smoke to tenderize and flavor meats and vegetables. Like grills, smokers can be fueled by charcoal, like the one shown *at far left,* or by gas, like the combination grill/smoker *at near upper left.*

All outdoor cookers should be cleaned after each use and protected from the elements. Line a charcoal grill with heavy foil for easy ash disposal.

OUTFITTING YOUR YARD

It's a warm summer evening and the aroma of barbecued hamburgers fills the air. The party's about to begin when uninvited guests arrive—flies, moths, mosquitoes, or ants. Don't despair. Effective pest control *is* available—in both chemical and non-chemical modes. Cooler weather poses a different sort of problem—one that a portable heater just might solve.

HEATERS AND PEST CONTROLS

In the battle of the bug, you have an arsenal of weapons to choose from, all of which fall into two general categories—chemical and non-chemical.

• *Chemical insecticides*, in powdered or liquid form, are usually mixed with water, then sprayed. One of the simplest applicators is a refillable bottle or tank with a handle on top that you use to build up pressure manually before spraying. Our photo shows two versions. Flanking the smaller one are two battery-operated items, a fogger, *left,* and a sprayer, *right.* Most home sprayers have vinyl tanks, which are lighter and easier to clean than metal tanks.

• *Non-chemical pest killers* work in a variety of ways. Some electronic units use "black light" to attract bugs, then zap them with a shot of high-voltage electricity. (One of these is hanging in the upper left corner of the photo.) Other models use water to drown the insects. The most effective units use fluorescent tubes that protect areas up to one-third of an acre.

Cool weather also discourages pests, but it may chase you indoors, too. *Outdoor heaters* will take the chill off an enclosed porch or greenhouse, or help warm up swimmers after a late-night dip. Catalytic heaters use either white gas or propane fuel. They operate from five to 60 hours without needing to be refilled. Electric units plug into an ordinary outlet.

OUTFITTING YOUR YARD

WATERING SYSTEMS

Regularly deep-watering your lawn, trees, and shrubs helps keep them flourishing and protects your landscaping investment. The problem is, most of us don't have the time or patience to hold a hose long enough to provide adequate water (at least an inch per week) over a large area. Help is available in a wide variety of watering systems, ranging from simple garden hoses with sprinkler attachments to soakers, drippers, and elaborate in-ground networks.

The basic watering tool is the hose. Typical ⅝-inch (inside diameter) hoses are made of vinyl or flexible rubber. Vinyl hoses are light and easy to handle; rubber versions are costly but more durable.

The most popular type of watering system uses a hose and a portable aboveground sprinkler attachment. Sprinklers come in stationary, rotating, oscillating, and walking models (like the tractor version shown here).

• *Specialized hose attachments* include showerheads, which deliver a rainlike spray; bubblers, which break the water's force into a gentle flow; foggers, which give a fine cooling mist; and spray guns for washing the car, screens, and house siding. Some of the adjustable nozzles provide several of these features. Besides traditional brass and aluminum attachments, you can select convenient snap-on plastic styles that are noncorrosive and shock-resistant.

• *Soakers*—perforated canvas or plastic hoses that deliver water along their length—let you deep-water right to plants' root zones, where the water does the most good. *Drip irrigation devices* usually consist of a raised header pipe connected to several lengths of thin, tapelike porous tubing that you unroll in the garden. Drip systems can cut water consumption by as much as 70 percent because little is lost to evaporation or runoff.

• *In-ground sprinkler systems* (available with both manual and automatic controls) are more efficient and timesaving than aboveground sprinklers. Durable PVC pipe and fittings are easy to assemble, and installing the system yourself cuts down on the expense considerably.

OUTFITTING YOUR YARD

Nightfall needn't be a signal to pack up and go inside. If you turn on the lights outdoors, your yard can be as dramatic and inviting at night as it is during the day. Well-planned lighting lets you use your yard full-time, and, at the same time, improves your home's security and safety.

LIGHTING

Too often, exterior lighting systems consist of nothing more than an entry lamp and a glaring floodlight or two—hardly the best way to take advantage of the dramatic possibilities that a well-designed outdoor illumination scheme can offer.

You may need assistance from a professional landscape designer and electrician, but with planning and know-how you can probably do most of the work yourself.

• *Entrance lighting* is a top priority for safety and security. Use a pair of wall brackets—one on each side of the main entry door. For safety, mount them about 66 inches above the top of the entrance steps. For a soft effect, shield fixtures with an 8-inch or larger enclosure. At other doors, mount one fixture on the lock side.

• *Walks or driveways* leading to a door can be lit with a post lantern. Shield the fixture so it won't temporarily blind approaching drivers. Then add some low-level fixtures along the path to the house.

Bright ideas

You can create dramatic accents with uplighting or downlighting. Fixtures mounted on the ground can direct light up through trees and shrubs, or along a fence, with magical results. Try suspending a canister light high in a tree, creating a shadowy moonlit aura. Or downlight flower gardens and paths with low mushroom-style fixtures.

• *Floodlights* are useful for lighting larger areas. Try mounting single or double weatherproof adjustable floods under the eaves or roof overhang. Use a 150-watt PAR-38 lamp to cover a large area at reasonable cost.

• *Perimeter lighting* is one of the most effective ways to light a deck or patio. Position lamps to spread light on the shrubs and flowers, with less intense light shed on the deck or patio area.

Outdoor lighting should be operable for long hours. High Intensity Discharge (HID) lamps give the most light per watt. Mercury lamps are a good choice, with low installation cost and a range of sizes from 40 to 250 watts.

Low-voltage lighting

Low-voltage systems like the one pictured *at left* offer an alternative to standard outdoor lighting. Their low-wattage bulbs use less energy than a 120-volt system, making them cheaper to operate. They are also easier to install. And they're safer because they operate with a transformer that converts household current to just 12 volts.

The transformer plugs into a weatherproof household outlet. From it, cables run to the areas you wish to light. The cables can be safely left above the ground or buried. Fixtures clip onto the cables and can be moved easily. (For more details about outdoor wiring, see page 143.)

You can select from among a variety of decorative fixtures, including 4-foot-tall post lights, 2-foot-high mushroom-shape path lights, and small ground-level spots and uplights. Some sets come with a choice of lens colors and automatic timing controls.

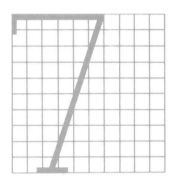

SPECIAL EXTRAS

With a little imagination, you can turn an ordinary yard into a highly personalized mini-vacation spot, a place for play and relaxation, a refuge from the demands of everyday life. Whether the special extra you dream of is a swimming pool, a putting green, or a play area for your children, it will require careful planning to create. Is it compatible with your family's needs? Will it still complement your life-style a few years from now? Will it affect resale value? And will your special extra be in compliance with local zoning and other codes?

HOT TUBS AND SPAS

Hot tubs and spas can be installed indoors, but their greatest appeal may be as luxurious spots for soothing, refreshing hot-water soaks in an outdoor setting.

Once you decide to install an outdoor hot tub or spa, you'll have to determine *where* to place it, based on these basic factors: compatibility with existing landscaping; access to existing water and electrical service; whether you prefer a sunny or a shady location; whether an open air setting will work or you'll need some sort of protective covering; wind patterns; views from inside the tub or spa; and privacy. For minimal privacy, construct an arbor, trellis, or fence.

The kind of setting—deck, patio, or apron—that you create will depend on the amount of space you have and the appearance of your present landscaping. Also, decide whether you'll need a walkway leading to the new fixture from your original outdoor living area and directly from the house. The installation shown *opposite* is approached via a curving path defined by a pair of benches that match the one on the deck. Be sure to plan space for heaters, filters, and other maintenance equipment, just as you would for a swimming pool.

Working with a kit, you should be able to put together a hot tub or spa by yourself in a few days. Most kits come complete with just about everything you'll need: plumbing and heating units, a pump, a filter, floor support piers, seats (usually), a lint trap, and a chlorine testing kit. Local building codes may require that you bring in a professional electrician or plumber to complete the installation; even if you're not required to do so, it's a good idea for safety reasons.

An average-size hot tub or spa—about 4x5 feet—holds about 475 gallons of water. When the tub is in use, you'll probably want the water to be at least 100 degrees Fahrenheit; when it's not in use, set the thermostat at 80 degrees to keep reheating time down. Naturally, heating this much water will add to your monthly utility bill. Thermal blankets and tub covers will help keep water-heating costs down.

Water and chlorine costs also should be part of your projected budget. Most people change the water in a hot tub or spa two or three times a year. The filter and the chlorine keep the tub or spa clean between changes.

Hot tubs and spas are not inexpensive; an average kit costs in the low thousands. Hot tubs are usually made of redwood, but teak, mahogany, cypress, and oak are also used. Spas are made of fiber glass or, occasionally, Gunite, a pneumatically applied concrete. Spas also offer a greater selection of shapes and colors than hot tubs do.

When you look at spas, make sure that there are no hairline cracks or other flaws. Look for reinforcing at the bottom, outlet, and steps.

Safety is a very important consideration with a hot tub or spa. Don't allow the water to become dangerously hot. Care for your hot tub as you would a swimming pool; deep water deserves to be treated with respect. Perhaps the most important advice to heed: Follow manufacturers' instructions carefully when you build and install your tub or spa; make sure everything is hooked up properly—and then enjoy yourself.

SWIMMING POOLS

A swimming pool in your own backyard may sound like an unjustifiable luxury. But consider the pleasures of before-breakfast dips, sun-time splashing, and moonlit swims—not to mention the exercise benefits—and a pool of your own may begin to make more sense. What's more, pool prices vary more widely than you might think. Here's what you need to know to decide whether—or how—to get into the swim.

Before you take the pool-building plunge, decide what you can afford to spend, keeping in mind that the cost of the pool itself is typically only about 60 percent of the total cost of pool ownership. Plan for the expenses of maintenance equipment, apron (the walking area surrounding the pool), fences, landscaping, and insurance, as well.

No matter what your budget, seeking professional help is a good idea—a skilled designer and/or builder can assure that the appearance, function, and cost of your new backyard "resort" will be all you hoped for. Get references and find out if a contractor is a member of the National Spa and Pool Institute, an organization that promotes guidelines for pool quality and safety standards.

Aboveground or in it?
Your first choice may be a traditional in-ground pool—until you discover what excavation and construction will cost.

More economical aboveground pool kits come in a variety of construction styles. The least expensive is a circular, continuous wall of lightweight sheet metal, but stronger versions have heavy, interlocking metal panels.

By partially setting an aboveground pool into a slope and surrounding it with an attractive deck like the one shown *at right*, you can camouflage its height and create delightful lazing space.

If you do decide to build an in-ground pool, explore these construction and style options.
- A *vinyl-lined* pool is likely to be the least expensive, and the least difficult project for do-it-yourselfers.
- *Concrete* is generally more durable, but usually requires skilled labor.

- *Fiber glass* and *metal* are other possibilities.
- *Shape*, especially with concrete pools, is just about unlimited—from the familiar rectangles, kidneys, or ovals to free-form designs.
- Other pool components to consider include the *interior finish*, the *trim* around the water line, the *coping* around the edge of the pool, *ladders* and *grab rails*, *diving* and *jumping equipment*, *underwater lights*, and *floating ropes* to mark off diving or swimming areas. You also may want a cover to protect your pool in cool weather or when the pool's not in use for long periods of time.

Fitting a pool into your yard
Few yards are too small or too steep to accommodate a pool. If a standard shape won't fit, you can custom-design a pool to suit your site. It will cost more, but an imaginative design can overcome the disadvantages of a hillside lot or postage-stamp corner.

If your lot is spacious, where you put a pool is still important. Remember to plan for access and storage for pool maintenance equipment.

Pool landscaping must be as practical as it is attractive.
- The *apron* may be grass, concrete, brick, wood, or aggregate. Whatever material you choose should provide not just a pleasant sunning surface but a safe, nonskid walkway. The apron also serves as a buffer to protect nearby plants from pool chemicals.
- Other vital safety features are *lockable gates* and sturdy *fences*—good for added privacy, too. Your insurance agent may have further suggestions.

GAZEBOS

What is a gazebo? Its very name evokes images of lazy summer days and moonlit nights, an idyllic refuge at the end of a shady garden, away from your everyday life. In less romantic terms, a gazebo is a post-and-beam structure, usually with five, six, or eight sides, and topped with a pitched roof. Enormously popular in the Victorian era, gazebos are once again in demand, and can be truly special places to escape, or to entertain.

A gazebo can be a teahouse or an outdoor party room, a poolside retreat or a secluded place in the shade. How you plan to use your gazebo will guide you in determining its shape, size, style, and location. If it's built properly, the gazebo will integrate your yard into your homelife by tempting you out of doors, not to rake or weed, but to relax and enjoy.

Gazebos can be attached or freestanding, and prefabricated units are available in many styles. For example, the airy and rather contemporary gazebo *opposite* is built into a deck; the charming freestanding Victorian *at right* is highlighted by an elaborate finial.

What will it look like?
Plan your gazebo to attract without being distracting. Whether it's to be open, screened, or glazed, round, hexagonal, or even square, make sure your gazebo is solidly constructed. New or salvage lumber is an obvious choice, but wrought iron, lath, concrete, or brick are other possibilities. The roof can be solid, trellis, lath, thatched, tiled, or covered with shakes, shingles, copper, or tin. Floors, too, offer lots of scope for your imagination. Gravel, wood, flagstone, tile, concrete, slate, brick, and bark chips all work well in the right setting. (For more about exterior materials in general, see pages 48-63.)

Carved scrollwork, or "gingerbread," is a hallmark of the classic Victorian gazebo. For a touch of charm and whimsy, add scrollwork under the eaves, on gable ends, railings, posts, doorways, and around windows. Lattice is another legacy from years gone by and another instant source of period appeal. A finial (a capping ornament) or a weather

vane of copper, wood, or wrought iron provides a nice finishing touch.

Planning
Whether you intend to build your gazebo or hire a contractor, plan carefully *before* you start. Consider wind, shade, sun patterns, nearness to neighbors (check any local ordinances about new structures near lot lines), and views. Also find out whether you'll need a building permit.
• If you plan to use the gazebo as an outdoor dining room, make sure it is near, or easily accessible to, your kitchen.
• When you decide on the material for your gazebo, consider ease of maintenance and

durability. Lumber should be treated or– like redwood— naturally resistant to insects, decay, and weathering. Remember, too, that if you decide to paint your gazebo, it will need more frequent attention than one left to weather.
• Extras like benches and built-in tables make a nice place a special place.
• Make sure there's easy access to the gazebo, if it's freestanding. The path leading to the gazebo should be inviting: A winding path will add to the gazebo's charm.

GAME AND PLAY AREAS

If your children often lament that "there's nothing to do around here"—and if you'd like a little recreation yourself—look around. You can make a safe, inviting play area for children or adults right, as the saying goes, in your own backyard. Here and on pages 116 and 117 are just a few of the myriad possibilities.

Depending on the ages of your family members and their outdoor interests, you can turn your yard into just about anything from a children's playground to a court where you can sharpen your tennis skills. With imagination and work, plus some regard for space and terrain, you'll be surprised at how much fun your yard can offer. (Another advantage: You never again have to mow the area you blacktop or concrete!)

Begin by listing all favorite family activities. Whether your priority is a basketball court or a playhouse with a slide obviously depends on the ages of your children as well as your own tastes. Take into account that needs can change, too.

Once you've determined what your family could best use—and enjoy—in the way of outdoor play space, think about where the facilities should be located. If space is limited, use a narrow side

yard, for example, to create a shuffleboard court like the one *below,* a sheltered play area, or a miniature putting green.

The all-purpose play area shown *at right* demonstrates that you can accommodate a variety of activities on an average-size city lot. The versatile design is good for basketball, hopscotch, and all other hard-surface games. Metal pipes set in asphalt let participants set up or remove poles and stakes for other activities, including tetherball and horseshoes. The bench in the foreground provides a resting spot, and protects plants, too.

Whatever you're constructing, location is a primary consideration. Is the activity better suited for sun or shade? Do you need a flat site or a gentle slope? Will you have to dig out the whole backyard, or just fence off a corner? The chart on page 117 can help you define space requirements.

(continued)

GAME AND PLAY AREAS
(continued)

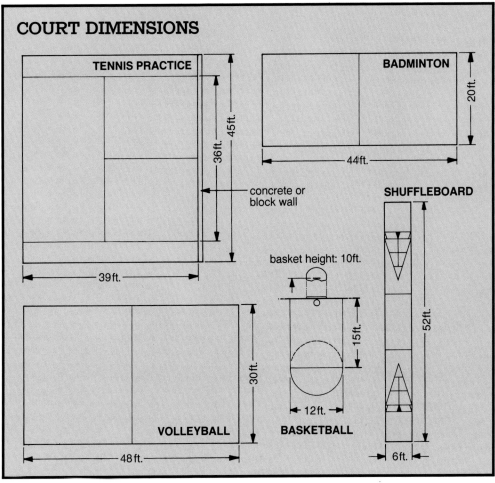

COURT DIMENSIONS

TENNIS PRACTICE

45 ft.

36 ft.

39 ft.

concrete or block wall

BADMINTON

20 ft.

44 ft.

SHUFFLEBOARD

52 ft.

6 ft.

basket height: 10 ft.

15 ft.

12 ft.

BASKETBALL

VOLLEYBALL

30 ft.

48 ft.

A place to climb or swing or let off steam lures children as reliably as an ice-cream truck bell. The photograph *at left* shows how one small space, when transformed with simple, inexpensive materials, can become an inviting play center.

Safety is a key consideration for children's play equipment. No sharp corners or protruding hardware should be evident anywhere. A good foundation system, anchored in concrete for stability, is also a must for climbing equipment or swings. Check all surfaces for splinters and rough edges, and sand them if necessary.

If you build a game court, select a surface suitable to your planned activities. For basketball or tennis, asphalt, concrete, or clay will work best. For golf, try artificial turf instead of grass. Sand or bark chips cushion landings under play structures. With any materials, consider weather resistance as well as safety. (See pages 48 to 63 for more about materials; pages 134 and 135 show children's projects.)

Don't try to grow delicate plants or flowers around a game or play area. The low-maintenance plants that stand up to children, tossed balls, and pets are the best choice.

You may want to build a wood or wire fence or screen, or create a living fence with hardy plants to help keep youngsters and balls in the play space and out of your neighbors' yards.

Some play areas require little construction work. Badminton, volleyball, tetherball, croquet, and horseshoes need a level space but require minimum site preparation. Tennis, handball, paddleball, and other racket sports must be played on a hard surface surrounded by some type of fencing. The box *above* shows typical dimensions for court games.

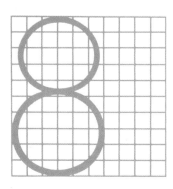

HOW DOES YOUR GARDEN GROW?

Beginning gardeners like to visualize their yards rich with thriving flowers and plants from earliest spring until killing frost—even year-round in mild-winter zones. But most gardeners soon discover that no single plant is at its best for a full 12 months. With a little planning, though, you can grow combinations of flowers that will take turns providing color. Even if you have only a tiny corner or strip of earth, you can grow two or three kinds of plants together. Gardening offers more than just lovely flowers. Vegetables, herbs, and even wildlife add to the pleasures of gardening. In this chapter, we'll show you how to start getting the most out of your garden.

IN THE SPRING AND SUMMER

A spring and summer flower garden can give delight in the winter, too. Why? Because you have to plan before you plant—and leafing through seed catalogs can be almost as much fun as enjoying the end results.

Start your planning by choosing a location that will please both you and the flowers you want to plant. Try to find a space that receives at least six hours of full sun each day. If you can, make your floral borders 4 to 6 feet deep—for anything deeper, you'll need footpaths or stepping-stones to provide access for weeding, clipping faded flowers, and other maintenance chores. The length of your flower beds and borders depends on the space available and how much time and energy you want to expend.

Once you've found a promising site for your flower garden, draw a rough plot plan to a scale of ¼ to ½ inch per foot. (See pages 26-29 for more about plotting and planning your landscape.)

To determine what kinds of flowering plants do well in your area, do some preliminary research. Check the zone map on page 121 to find the approximate range of minimum temperatures where you live; some "hardy" plants are hardier than others. Look at several good gardening books and nursery catalogs and visit a few local nurseries.

Designing your flower beds

Once your basic research is done, choose one easily grown keynote plant for each growing season and one or more varieties to serve as fillers and accents. Write down, season by season, the low, medium, and tall plants you have chosen. Next draw informal circles to represent the

mature spread of each plant; you can even color the circles to approximate the expected hues.

Color is probably the most exciting part of flower gardening. In the spring bulb and the summer perennial borders shown *opposite*, several strong colors combine to make a brilliant display.

If you're planning your first flower garden, however, start with a relatively simple color scheme for each season. For example, plant your spring bulb garden with bright red early tulips accented by delicate bicolor daffodils like those shown in the inset *opposite left*. For a glowing hot-weather display, try zinnias in several warm shades; the red pompons in the inset *opposite right* are just one example of the brilliance these annuals can provide.

Overplant whenever you can. For example, set shallow-rooted annuals among deep-planted spring bulbs to take over as bulb foliage matures and withers.

Preparing and maintaining your flower bed

Most plants do best in loose, loamy soil. If your soil is sandy or clayey, work in some form of humus. Spade the bed at least 10 inches deep, turning the soil upside down as you return it to the bed to loosen and aerate the particles. When planting, firm the soil around each plant to eliminate air pockets. Water the plants immediately, then regularly until the new plants are firmly established.

Mulch your flower bed to cut down on weeding and to conserve soil moisture. Add extra mulch for winter protection, then remove it in the spring after the danger of frost has passed.

HOW DOES YOUR GARDEN GROW?

IN THE FALL

Globes of bright color, like the golden chrysanthemums in the inset *opposite*, are familiar September and October pleasures. Dahlias, sweet william, petunias, ageratum, marigolds, and violas—all dazzle beholders through and beyond the peak of hot weather. Many of these flowers may be right for your climate.

Other good candidates for late-season blooms include phlox, delphiniums, hollyhocks, veronica, balloon-flower, fall asters, orange butterfly weed, and autumn bulbs such as fall crocus, colchicum, and sternbergia. The shade-loving classics such as impatiens and begonias also last until late fall.

You can prolong the life of many of your flowering plants, chrysanthemums included, beyond the first few light frosts. When night temperatures drop only slightly and then rise rapidly during the day, you can protect plants overnight with old newspapers or sheets, weighted down so the wind won't blow them away. Plastic bags are not effective; cold penetrates them easily.

It's helpful to know when the first killing frost usually occurs in your area; ask your local weather bureau or county extension agent for assistance. Choose flower varieties that will bloom before the first killing frost. With a little care and planning, your fall garden will reward you with a spectacular late show.

How's the weather?

The zone map, *above*, compiled by the United States Department of Agriculture, tells how cold it gets in your part of the country—key information for determining which plants will grow well in your flower and vegetable gardens.

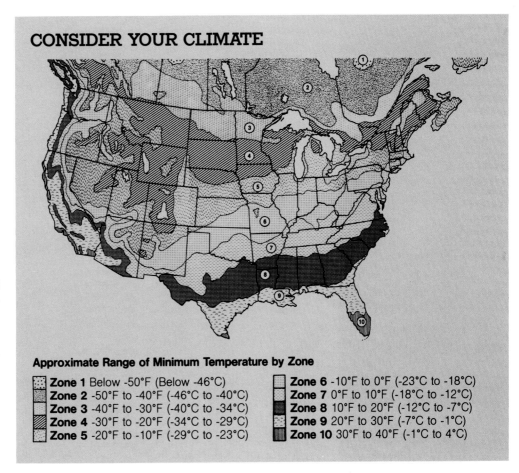

CONSIDER YOUR CLIMATE

Approximate Range of Minimum Temperature by Zone

Zone 1 Below -50°F (Below -46°C)	**Zone 6** -10°F to 0°F (-23°C to -18°C)
Zone 2 -50°F to -40°F (-46°C to -40°C)	**Zone 7** 0°F to 10°F (-18°C to -12°C)
Zone 3 -40°F to -30°F (-40°C to -34°C)	**Zone 8** 10°F to 20°F (-12°C to -7°C)
Zone 4 -30°F to -20°F (-34°C to -29°C)	**Zone 9** 20°F to 30°F (-7°C to -1°C)
Zone 5 -20°F to -10°F (-29°C to -23°C)	**Zone 10** 30°F to 40°F (-1°C to 4°C)

Other conditions to consider before selecting plants are average rainfall, humidity, snow coverage, wind, and soil type. Your state agricultural school or local county extension service can provide general information tailored to local needs. For example, a specific perennial may survive in Zone 3 in Maine but be completely unadapted to Zone 3 in North Dakota. The reason lies in the differences in rainfall and humidity in the two zones.

Also be sure to consider the mini-climate zones—those variations that exist on your own plot of ground. Land on the south side of your house, for instance, is bound to be warmer than a constantly shaded area that is exposed to cold, northwest winds. And an area that gets full, hot sun will dry out faster than a depression along a drainage route, even though the drainage route also gets lots of sun.

If you live in a snowy climate, note how snow piles up in your garden. Drifts, which can supply valuable extra water to underlying plants, are likely to last longer in the shade of a house, or where a structure or fence can deflect the winds.

Study the length of tree shadows in summer *and* winter. Avoid the disappointment of planting tomatoes or zinnias in what you're sure is a sunny patch, only to discover that with the trees in full leaf your garden area will encourage only impatiens.

Finally, be flexible. When certain plants do poorly, don't hesitate to replace them with hardier types. If others prosper unexpectedly, consider adding more of them—perhaps in additional varieties or colors.

121

WITH FLOWERS FOR CUTTING

Once you've established a flower garden, you'll be tempted to bring the beauty inside. To enjoy your own cut flowers and share them with friends without giving up the wealth of color outside, plant a cutting garden.

Usually, a cutting garden is a separate and relatively unseen piece of land set aside for growing indoor bouquets. It could be in a backyard, like the one *at right*, or simply tucked behind a taller flower bed that's intended for show. If space is tight, or if you simply don't have time to tend two distinct flower gardens, design a garden that's so well planned, varied, and abundant that flowers cut from carefully chosen sections won't be missed. Or, if you're really short on space, combine your cutting garden with your vege- table planting area.

With good planning, you can grow two cutting gardens on the same plot of land in one growing season. In the fall, plant a spring cutting garden of bulbs. When they blossom, plant annuals. By the time the annuals fill out and claim the space, the bulb foliage will have matured and withered.

The skillfully massed border *opposite* shows how a wealth of flowers can offer cutting opportunities in addition to a gala outdoor display. Here are some tips for creating your own cutting garden.
• Include perennials, biennials, and annuals, but be careful to place perennials where root systems won't be disturbed.
• Plant short-season annuals and tender bulbs every three weeks during planting season; that way you'll have a succes- sion of blooms. Try to select varieties that bloom at different times during a season.

• Plant in rows running north and south, to take greatest advantage of the sun as it moves from east to west.
• As with any flower garden, keep your cutting garden well watered to ensure a good crop of healthy, good-size blooms.
• Removing spent flower heads that you didn't cut will encourage the plants to produce another round of blossoms.

What to plant
Daffodils and tulips are basic choices for springtime bou- quets. Daffodils, or narcissus, will probably flower first. For variety, plant double narcissus, large-cupped narcissus, white color trumpets, and bicolor trumpets.

The array of colors available for tulip growers is exciting. When you're choosing colors for your cutting garden, think about what will look best inside your home.

With all bulbs, keep in mind that you have to let the foliage wither so the bulbs can build up strength for next year's flowering.

For summer cutting, you'll find that plants are in flower much sooner if they're set out as seedlings rather than sown from seed outdoors. Zinnias, marigolds, and dwarf dahlias are reliable and colorful summer flowers.

Drying flowers
A cutting garden also gives you the chance to put together long-lasting bouquets of dried flowers. Statice, lavender, and honesty are popular flowers for drying. To dry flowers, gather them at midday; don't pick flowers after a heavy rain or when they're covered with dew—mildew can form and make them rot. Strip the leaves from the stems; gather the stems together in bunches and bind them with plastic ties. Hang them upside down in a dark, well-ventilated place for at least three weeks.

HOW TO HANDLE CUT FLOWERS

Flowers remain alive after cutting, so it's important to give them proper treatment to help them take up and retain water.

Cut flowers at their coolest temperature. Avoid buds that are too tight—they will never fully open. Harvest the flowers that bloom in clusters when about half the blooms have opened. Flowers picked at full bloom have a short life expectancy.

For flowers with thick or woody stems, mash the ends or slit the base with a sharp knife, going upward for an inch or two, to help the stem take in more water.

Hollow stems or stems that secrete a milky substance when cut, such as those of poppies and dahlias, need to be seared with a flame when cut, then left in lukewarm water.

Clip off all leaves that are below the water level—they rot quickly and shorten the life of your flowers.

One additional tip—to keep flowers looking their best as long as possible, place finished arrangements away from drafts, hot light bulbs, and direct sunlight.

WITH FLOWERS IN CONTAINERS

Spectacular flower color can be yours even if outdoor space is severely limited. Choose the right plants, learn the basics of container gardening, and your walkway, patio, or postage-stamp flower bed can dazzle from spring until frost—or year-round if you live in a mild climate. As the deck *opposite* and the patio *at right* illustrate, potted plants can brighten every aspect of your outdoor living space.

For dependable, long-lasting color that looks much more expensive than it is, fill your pots with annuals. A packet of flower seeds is still one of the great American bargains. For a little more money and even less effort, you can buy flats of bedding plants, pot them, and achieve instant color.

The big four varieties among annuals—geraniums, marigolds, petunias, and zinnias—thrive in containers, as do many other equally colorful and rewarding species. Naturally, the more sun you have to offer your plants, the wider the range of varieties to choose from. In shady areas, impatiens and wax begonias will flower as reliably and colorfully in pots as they do in beds; try coleus and caladiums for interesting foliage. (Caution: Caladiums are poisonous, which makes them a poor choice for patios where pets or small children play.) Grow roses successfully in containers, as long as the pots provide good drainage and are big enough to accommodate the large root structures.

Strategically place two or three pots at corners of a patio or at your front entry for a dramatic and delightful impact. For a variation on freestanding potted plants, try window boxes. Flower-filled window boxes have their own special charm

and make almost any home look welcoming and cherished.

Planting in containers

For soil, buy a lightweight potting mix, or make your own with soil, peat moss, and perlite. Cover the bottom of the box with broken clay pot fragments, and add a layer of peat moss or nylon netting. Then fill the boxes with soil. Mix a handful of slow-release fertilizer to give the plants a good start. Moisten the soil thoroughly and set out the plants. For window boxes, you can either set all plants directly in the box or plant them in individual pots so they can be rearranged in the box.

Most container plants look best if placed fairly close together. Space low edging plants such as sweet alyssum, lobelia, and dwarf marigolds about 3 to 5 inches apart. Taller plants such as petunias thrive when planted 4 to 6 inches apart.

Keeping container plants at their best

Before using clay pots, soak the containers in water so the dry clay won't pull all the moisture from the soil. Even with this precaution, soil in clay pots dries out quickly, so check the soil surface often, and water when it feels dry.

Turn container plants occasionally to encourage symmetrical growth. Place pots where they won't be subjected to constant one-directional winds, which will bend them, or sudden gusts of wind, which may knock them over or break them. Plants that are weighted with sand mixed with the soil or are set in heavy containers to start with are better able to resist strong breezes. (To build your own sturdy planters, see pages 136 and 137.)

Keep annuals that have a tendency to get leggy—such as petunias and coleus— pinched back to encourage more compact growth. Once flowering starts, remove faded blooms regularly; if plants are allowed to go to seed, they will stop blooming.

PLANT SHELTERS

If you want fresh flowers and vegetables year-round, and a place to start seedlings in late winter, consider adding on a greenhouse. You can build your own if you're a do-it-yourselfer.

The greenhouse shown *opposite* serves as a decorative summer resort for houseplants and also provides a year-round supply of salad crops. The structure is framed with redwood boards and measures 4x8 feet. The glass roof panels are painted to diminish the glare. (For a practical greenhouse/ shed that you can build, see page 141.)

If you're short on time and/or skill, invest in a prefab greenhouse that can be installed in hours, not days. Most greenhouse manufacturers offer small, affordable units in an assortment of sizes and shapes.

A good plant protector for hot climates is a lath house, where plants can be left outdoors most of the year. A lath structure provides protection from hot sun, strong winds, and driving rains, and also allows for the benefits of filtered sunshine, good air circulation, and natural watering by rainfall. Potted houseplants will thrive during an outdoor summer vacation in a lath house.

WITH VEGETABLES

FIVE WAYS TO BOOST YIELDS

If your gardening space is limited, make wise use of what you have to get more from less. The trick is to become as familiar as possible with the specific cultivation needs of various crops. Here are some space-maximizing ideas to keep in mind.

• *Interplanting*. Rapid-growing vegetables such as radishes, lettuces, spinach, and scallions can be interspersed with long-season crops such as corn, cabbage, broccoli, winter squash, and tomatoes. The quick-growing crops will be harvested before the slower ones demand their full space allotment. You might also tuck some short-season vegetables among your flower seedlings.

• *Second cropping*. Some vegetables grow so fast that they are soon gone, and you're left with unproductive space. To avoid this, plant new crops as the old ones finish producing. For instance, when peas are done producing, pull the vines and use the same space to raise another fast-growing cool-season crop, such as carrots, cauliflower, spinach, or turnips.

• *Succession planting*. For a continuous harvest without wasteful surplus, plant short rows of crops at brief intervals. For example, plant several feet of lettuce. Two weeks later, sow another row, and in another 14 days, start a third. Radishes, mustard, chard, beans, and spinach make good succession plants.

With tomatoes, cabbage, corn, and melons, choose different varieties that mature early, mid-season, and late.

• *Vertical gardening*. Vegetables that grow on long, rambling vines, such as melons and cucumbers, are space guzzlers. But they're just as happy growing up as growing out and around. In fact, they may produce better that way: Off the ground they are cleaner and easier to pick, and perhaps less disease prone. If you don't have a sunny trellis, construct a tepee-like support and plant seeds at the base of the poles. Maturing squash and melons may become too heavy for the vertical vine to support, so tie the fruits up with slings made of netting or discarded nylon stockings. Keep tomatoes from sprawling by staking or caging them.

• *Mulching*. Add 4 to 6 inches of mulch in late spring to control weeds, hold moisture in the soil, and moderate soil temperatures. After the growing season ends, you can turn under an organic mulch; it will decompose and improve the structure of the soil. Favorite organic mulches include well-rotted compost, ground corncobs, clean straw, hay, sawdust, and shredded newspapers. Strips of black plastic can be used in place of an annual organic mulch.

Perhaps no gardening achievement is quite as satisfying as growing your own vegetables. Harvesting even a few juicy tomatoes or a handful of crunchy radishes is rewarding. The luxuriant garden plots *opposite* show backyard vegetable gardening raised to the level of art. Although a large garden may be your long-term goal, you can start with something much smaller and simpler.

Before you plant your garden, sit down with your family and decide what crops you really want to plant—and eat. If lettuce is a family favorite, plant several kinds. If nobody likes lima beans, even home-grown ones won't be popular.

Space and location
Some plants require much more space than others in proportion to their yield. For example, corn, though almost everyone's favorite, produces relatively few ears per square foot of garden. Tomatoes, on the other hand, produce pounds of delicious fruit in only a few square yards of space.

Location is of prime importance in planning—and planting—a vegetable garden. Vegetables need lots of sun: Warm-season crops such as melons, corn, and tomatoes need at least six hours of full sun each day for maximum growth. Plant tall crops, such as corn and pole beans, where they will not cast a shade over smaller plants. Perennials—asparagus and rhubarb for example—should get a spot that is free of traffic and undisturbed by the plow or the tiller.

Growing seasons
Different crops need to be planted at different times.
• *Long-season crops* take the entire season to grow, flower,

and produce mature fruit. Melons, winter squash, potatoes, pumpkins, peppers, and eggplants are in this group.

• *Short-season crops* can be sown and harvested before the season is half over, which means that several plantings can be made in one season. Radishes, beans, lettuce, and beets are some of the popular short-season crops.

• *Cool-season crops* can be planted as early in the spring as you can work the soil. Such crops include radishes, beets, broccoli, peas, potatoes, and onions.

• *Warm-season crops* should not be planted until the danger of frost is completely passed in your area. These crops include cucumbers, peppers, summer squash, tomatoes, beans, and watermelon.

Tools and soil
To prepare the ground for your vegetable garden, you'll need a garden tiller—either rent the machine or have the work done for you. You'll also need a few hand tools: a long-handled hoe, a steel rake, a watering can, a garden hose, twine, and a measuring stick.

The quality and nature of the soil are important to your garden's success. Most vegetables do best in slightly acid soil. To test for this, and for the soil's fertility, use a soil-testing kit, available from most garden supply stores. Your county extension office also can arrange for a test to be made at the nearest soil-testing station. Even the poorest soil is easily improved by adding compost, manure, and other organic matter.

WITH VEGETABLES
IN CONTAINERS
AND RAISED BEDS

You don't need an acre of land to enjoy your own fresh, homegrown vegetables. Potatoes will grow in bushel baskets, cherry tomatoes will thrive in hanging baskets, lettuce will produce lush green leaves in window boxes, and, by using raised beds, you can realize high yields in compact spaces.

To start a container garden, place your containers in any sunny spot: a patio, balcony, deck, flat rooftop as shown *at right*—even at the sides of wide steps. If you decide to garden on a balcony or rooftop, make sure it can support the weight of heavy pots, which weigh even more when watered.

Container soil dries out quickly, because, unlike topsoil, it can't soak up moisture from the water table. Thus, it's important to water container vegetables frequently—every day in hot, dry weather—and make sure that the soil you use retains water well. Sand holds practically no water. Add peat moss, perlite, vermiculite, or rotted compost to help soil retain water.

If you need small amounts of container soil, purchase specially prepared mixes. Investigate the synthetic soils that are available—all have been developed to provide everything plants need for good growth.

For larger amounts of soil, consider mixing your own. The basic ingredients are equal amounts of garden loam, peat moss, and coarse builders' sand. If your garden soil is sandy, you will need to reduce or eliminate the sand portion.

Anything that holds soil can be a garden container. Cake pans, plastic hampers, wood baskets, clay pots—even an old sink—will do. Or, build your own wooden containers.

128

The mobile mini-garden *at upper left* is easy to construct from treated lumber. Casters on the four corners let you easily roll the structure to pockets of sun that vary with the time of year, or even time of day. The seven-tier design accommodates six-foot rows of spinach, romaine and leaf lettuces, basil, radishes, green onions, and, on the bottom deck, bush cucumbers.

To shield plants from too-hot sun, unroll black plastic that has been stapled across the top of the structure. An inch of gravel in the base of each 8-inch-deep trough provides drainage.

Raised beds

Proper soil preparation is the key to successful gardening, and raised beds are no exception. Raised beds are just what they sound like—they're higher than the area surrounding them because the soil is well worked. In the raised-bed garden *at lower left*, peas and beans climb strings to further conserve space.

To construct a raised bed, first mark off the location of each 4-foot-wide bed with twine. Separate beds with 1-foot-wide paths. Use a sharp spade to turn over the soil to a depth of 12 inches. As you turn it, remove rocks, weeds, grass, and other debris.

Raised beds are permanent—there's no need to redig or till every spring, as a flat garden requires. And raised beds dry out sooner in the spring, so you can get a head start on the season. (They also dry out faster in the summer, of course, so frequent watering is a must.)

WITH HERBS

USING HERBS

Herbs have had many uses throughout the ages. Some were once believed to have magical powers; others have long been used for cooking and medicinal purposes. Herbs that are almost indispensable for flavoring include parsley, chives, sage, thyme, basil, spearmint, and marjoram.

• *Teas*. Many herbs, alone and in combination with each other, make refreshing teas. Some are made with dried leaves; others are taken from flower heads. Chamomile, comfrey, lemon balm, the mints, rosemary, and scented geraniums are some of the herbs that can be used to make tea.

• *Fragrance*. Aromatic herbs provide ingredients for sweet-scented potpourris and sachets. Lavender is probably the best known of the fragrant herbs. There are three kinds of lavender. English lavender is the showiest and has the most fragrant flowers, French lavender is used as a bath scent, and spike lavender produces large and fragrant leaves. Other especially fragrant herbs include sage, rosemary, lemon verbena, chamomile, and mint.

Parsley, sage, rosemary, and thyme are only the familiar beginning of a long list of herbs that can grace your garden. And, with a garden of herbs to choose from, you can try your hand at unusual flavorings, exotic teas, dried decorative arrangements, even potpourri. Reliable and versatile, herbs demand little except sunshine and good drainage.

Traditionally, herbs were grown in formal, geometrically arranged gardens. Informal arrangements can be just as pleasing, however. The lush herb garden *at right* combines a little of both styles.

Perennial favorites and others

Herbs offer a variety of gardening choices. Use them as edgings, as focal points, even as ground covers. Creeping thyme or chamomile, for example, used as a border adjacent to a lawn or walkway, will scent the air deliciously when trampled or clipped by the lawn mower.

Many herbs come back every year, which makes them true perennials. Some, such as mint, are so persistent that they will invade your garden if given half a chance. To control their growth, contain their roots in large cans submerged in earth with their bottoms cut out, or use sunken drainage tiles. Other herbs (marjoram, for instance) are perennial in mild climates but will not survive harsh winters and should be protected by thick mulch. Annual herbs, which include dill, chervil, fennel, basil, and parsley, often reseed themselves each year.

If full sun is hard to come by in your gardening space, try growing sweet woodruff, an excellent ground cover whose patterned leaves are used as

an essential ingredient in May wine. Lovage, good in salads, soups, and stews, can tolerate some shade but needs rich soil. The mint family, with all its variety of flavor and fragrance, thrives in shade. Oregano, chervil, and parsley also grow in partial shade.

Container herb gardening

If you are limited to gardening in containers, be sure to include herbs. Set out plants in individual pots, or try a small collection of cooking herbs in a window box or tub. The light-weight fiber pots in the inset *opposite* are filled with parsley, mint, celery, dill, and lavender.

Like all container-grown plants, herbs need good drainage. Fill pots with a layer of pottery shards or fine gravel and an inch or two of peat or sphagnum moss. Top off the container with soil mix, and water thoroughly before planting, so the soil settles.

If you plan to start your container herbs from seed, sow them directly in the pot you plan to grow them in. To do this, scatter herb seeds over the soil and cover them with a very thin layer of sand. To conserve moisture, lay a piece of glass or plastic over the top of the pot. Most seeds need darkness to germinate, so keep the pots in a dark place or cover them with card-board. As soon as the seedlings emerge, remove the cover and place the pots in a sunny location. Thin the plants when they're 3 or 4 inches high, leaving one to three plants per pot, depending on the size of your container.

WITH WILDLIFE

PEACEFUL COEXISTENCE

Delightful as it is to have flocks of birds and families of small animals visit regularly, you may want to keep them away from some parts of your garden.

Many heavily blooming and fruit-bearing shrubs and trees are big favorites with birds. To keep them from devouring your strawberries, raspberries, or cherries, plant a few mulberry, serviceberry, or elderberry bushes for them; Virginia creeper may divert the birds from grapes. You also can protect your trees with netting. Hanging a piece of suet a safe distance from your garden may satisfy birds' hunger before they discover your crops.

If you're trying to grow vegetables, screen the crops with wire-mesh and lath boxes to discourage greedy ground creatures such as squirrels. Or try folk remedies to protect your tender growing flowers and plants from rabbits and squirrels. Some people sprinkle red pepper on blossoms they would like small animals to ignore; other people try moth balls or dried blood, which is available at garden centers. Whatever deterrent you use, be especially careful not to endanger children and domestic animals, or the soil.

The same trees, shrubs, and flowering plants that make your garden beautiful and inviting also provide food and shelter for the wild creatures in your area.

Food and water
All creatures need water, for bathing as well as drinking. Birdbaths and shallow saucers are good water containers. For birds, place the container near shrubs or other tall plants; birds like to have an "escape" perch close-by. Make squirrels and other small climbers welcome *and* happy by providing ground-level supplies to prevent the animals from competing with and disturbing the birds. Keep water bowls and feeders away from overhanging limbs or beams from which cats may leap.

Add a small recirculating pool like the one *above* and *opposite* to grow aquatic plants such as hardy water lilies and cattails. Not only will you be able to raise fish, but you'll also attract frogs and turtles. Add rocks in and around the pool so these amphibians and reptiles can sun themselves. (For more information about pools and water gardens, see pages 44 and 45.)

Fruit-, nectar-, and seed-producing species attract wildlife. But until your plants are well established, place bird feeders throughout the garden and fill them with mixed seeds and other treats. Once seed-producing plants are established, supplemental feedings will no longer be necessary.

Shelter and open space
Birds and small animals, such as the chipmunk in the inset *opposite,* need protection from predators and weather. For example, a rock pile is a haven for toads and other tiny creatures, hawthorn is a good site for birds' nests, and white spruce provides winter cover.

If you're starting with a bare site covered only with grass, include a few man-made shelters—a pile of brush, a rock wall, even a compost heap.

Birds and squirrels nest in a wide variety of trees and shrubs. Some bird species prefer nest boxes, so provide some birdhouses.

Shelter is important, but so is open space. A grassy area tempts worm-hunting robins, for example, and also gives a good view of your visitors.

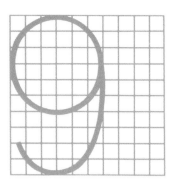

YARD PROJECTS YOU CAN BUILD

The right finishing touches can make your yard more functional, and more fun. Large and small, practical and whimsical, these projects can be custom-tailored to your family's needs. On the next 12 pages you'll find projects ranging from a play structure for kids to a greenhouse storage shed, and from dramatic lighting and handsome planters to benches, bird feeders, and more. Construct any of these projects as presented, or use them as starting points for any of your own favorite designs.

FOR KIDS

Bring the playground to your own backyard with a super play structure no kid can resist. A backyard jungle gym offers a great escape for children and, at the same time, helps develop important coordination skills. As the children get older, swings can be replaced with bars and rings for gymnastics and body building workouts. Both teens and adults can chin themselves using the top rungs of the structure.

A playtime project like the one shown *opposite* is easy to build and maintain, and it will fit into any yard, even a tiny one. This unit is constructed of redwood, but you also can use pressure-treated lumber. As the drawing *below* shows, strongly braced 2x4s are the main structural elements. The design combines a sandbox, old-fashioned rope-hung tire swing, sling swing, ladders, and jungle-gym bars. For extra design interest and dimension,

the ¾-inch dowels of the ladder sections extend 1½ inches beyond the side rails.

For stability, uprights are attached to two horizontal 2x4s on the ground. The wooden curb of 1x10s is capped with 1x6s to form an edging, provide seating for small-size spectators, and to separate the sand box from the adjoining flower beds.

Build each of the gym's main components on the ground, securing joints with galvanized lag bolts, then call in a few friends to help raise the triangular sections and connect them with the horizontal ladder.

Keep safety in mind when planning any play structure. Sand, grass, or other soft surfaces promise easy landings for young acrobats. To further minimize the chances of injury, avoid building pointed objects, protrusions, rough surfaces, and sharp edges into the structure.

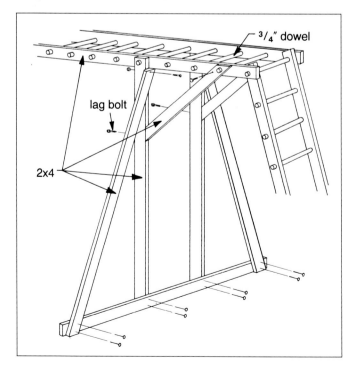

PLANTERS

Splash color around the deck, patio, pool, and yard with planters that go where you want them to. Fill planters with your favorite flowering annuals to create an instant portable garden, then strategically place them to screen an unsightly view, form a privacy barrier, or add a welcome accent. Here's a group of planters—variations on the basic box—with a dash of individuality. If you design your own planters, raise them slightly off the ground so air can circulate beneath them. Flowers in planters tend to dry out quickly, so keep your plants in picture-perfect shape with frequent watering and pruning. Move your planters as needed for proper sun exposure.

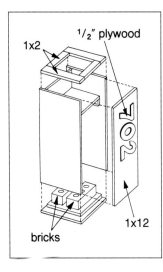

Everyone should spot your house number at a glance when it's mounted on a planter. A striking idea for dressing up an entry or driveway, the planter *at right* uses a sturdy post built of redwood 1x12s. One-inch scraps set behind the oversized house numbers raise them, creating a three-dimensional effect. Edge the planter top with 1x2s, and add a shelf to hold potted plants. Drill drainage holes in the shelf and apply stain or sealant, if desired.

One sheet of 4x8-foot exterior plywood siding will yield several handsome planters. Start with a framework of 1x2s and attach 18-inch-square sections of siding with non-corrosive nails and waterproof glue. Install a false bottom partway up in each box so less soil will be required to fill the planters. Drill drainage holes in the bottom, apply a sealant to all raw edges, and spread a ½- to 1-inch layer of crushed rock in each bottom. Add potting soil up to an inch below the top. Fill the planters with annuals, spacing 4 to 6 inches apart.

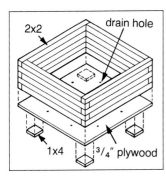

2x2

drain hole

1x4   ³/₄" plywood

Like a log cabin, these planters are built with overlapping ends to stabilize the corners. Redwood 2x2s nailed together form the sides; a piece of ¾-inch exterior-grade plywood, drilled with ½-inch drainage holes, forms the bottom. The planters are 24 inches square, but you can adjust the measurements to build larger or smaller planters. Apply stain to the outside and coat the bottom with polyester resin.

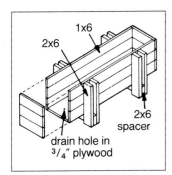

1x6

2x6

2x6 spacer

drain hole in ³/₄" plywood

This planter offers contemporary styling. Here, the beauty of the wood vies with the flowers for attention. The sides of the boxes are each built of three 1x6s. The legs are made of 2x6s that wrap around the planters. Use exterior-grade plywood for the bottom, and drill drainage holes. The planters work well singly or grouped as shown.

SEATING

When you feel the need to relax, what better retreat can you turn to than an outdoor seat? Enjoy a quiet moment there or laze away an entire summer evening reading, chatting, or just dozing. Your secret fantasy may be an old-fashioned porch swing or a secluded backyard bench nestled among fragrant flowers. No matter what your choice, attractive seating will add comfort to your outdoor living, and building your own can save you money.

SEATING

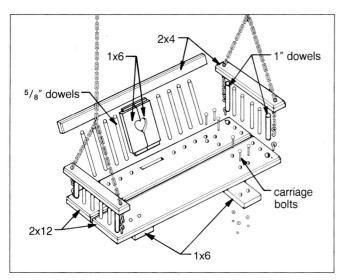

5/8" dowels
1x6
2x4
1" dowels
carriage bolts
2x12
1x6

An outdoor retreat needn't be elaborately designed; a bench or swing in the right place may be all you need. Place seating where you can enjoy special features on your property—a particularly attractive view or a shady, secluded spot, for example.

An old-fashioned porch swing brings memories of warm summer evenings—real or imagined—at Grandma's house. In the days before air conditioning, porch swings were standard equipment for most homes. Today, they're once again a popular outdoor retreat. Even if you don't have a porch, you can adapt by suspending a swing from an overhead structure.

To build a swing like the one shown *opposite*, begin by cutting two 47-inch-long 2x12s for the seat. Place them side by side, and join them by attaching two lengths of 1x6s across the underside with carriage bolts. Drill holes in the ends of the seat for arm-support dowels—you'll need a 1-inch dowel at the ends of each arm and four 5/8-inch dowels between. Cut 22-inch 2x4s for

the arms; drill holes for the dowels and a 1-inch hole in each end to receive the hanging chain. Cut dowels to 8½ inches and glue in place.

Cut a 43-inch 2x4 for the back. Cut two 14-inch 1x6s for the center panel and make the heart-shaped cutout with a saber saw. Cut a 20-degree mortise for the seat and a 90-degree mortise for the back. Cut panel tenons to fit each mortise.

Cut eight 14-inch-long 5/8-inch dowels for the back. Drill the seat and underside of the back for the dowels. Angle the holes in the seat at 20 degrees. Glue dowels and panel in place.

Attach four eyebolts in the corners of the seat. Thread two 96-inch lengths of chain from bolts at the front of the seat through holes in the arms and to bolts at the back. Attach lengths of chain at the middle and to the eyebolts with S-hooks; hang from ceiling joists or overhead supports. Make sure that the hardware you select and the structure that you hang the swing from can support the weight of the swing and two people.

Here's an example, *below*, of how a little ingenuity coupled with an unusual material can create attractive, inexpensive, and easy-to-build outdoor seating.

The garden bench is sturdy and simple to make. It's not the heavyweight it appears to be; the supports are inexpensive, commercial, concrete flue liners made of lightweight pumice. Available in many sizes, they can be used for a variety of projects, including planters, benches, compartmentalized storage, and tables.

To assemble the bench, you'll need a drill that's equipped with a concrete bit.

Begin by drilling through the pumice and plank, then secure the plank to the flue liners with four carriage bolts. Plane the long edges of the planks into a curve that matches the curve of the flue, as shown in the illustration *below*.

Stain and finish the wood, unless you use cedar or redwood, which can be left unfinished to weather to a pleasing gray shade.

A pedestal of stacked flue liners provides a firm base for a table to go with your bench. Top with your choice of material—laminated wood or smoked acrylic, for example, cut in any shape you desire.

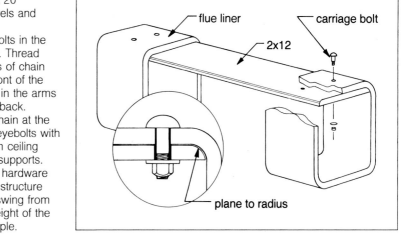

flue liner
carriage bolt
2x12
plane to radius

SHEDS
AND MORE

If shelter for garden and recreation equipment or outdoor furniture tops your list of needed backyard improvements, think beyond the traditional shed. For the same cost in labor and materials (or only slightly more), you can build a multipurpose unit—a solution for all your outdoor storage needs. Here we show just two examples of the versatile shed: a playhouse plus storage shed and a greenhouse storage unit. You can come up with other variations on the basic theme, such as a screened picnic shelter/shed or a workshop shed. Just be sure to check local building codes before you begin construction.

Yesterday's rustic backyard sheds have been replaced in many yards by prefabricated metal storage sheds. If neither of those alternatives appeals to you, one of these versatile storage ideas may.

Even though the main function of most sheds is to provide convenient storage for garden tools, firewood, and the family's recreational equipment, a shed can offer much more than just storage space. The two examples on these pages lead double lives, and the extra effort to design and build them pays off in their dual usefulness.

The playhouse-plus shown *at left* is a double-decker delight for the neighborhood kids and a spacious storehouse for lawn furniture, bikes, and garden equipment. Vary the dimensions to suit your requirements. This structure measures 6x12 feet. The overhanging tree house is equipped with its own ladder, balcony, and windows for light and ventilation. A simple wiring job could provide light to the playroom and shed, if desired.

The foundation of concrete footings supports an exterior-grade plywood floor. Framing is 2x4 studs with 2x6 rafters. Finish off the interior with plywood if you like. Outside, use exterior plywood or lumber siding, with asphalt shingles, wood shakes, or wood shingles as roofing. Cedar or redwood siding may be left unfinished to weather naturally. Other types of siding should be painted or stained.

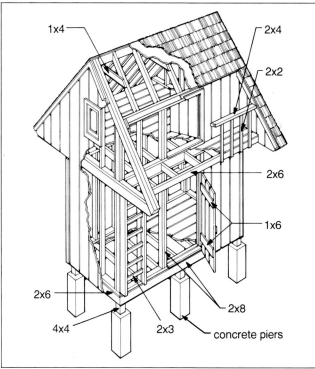

1x4 — 2x4 — 2x2 — 2x6 — 1x6 — 2x6 — 4x4 — 2x3 — 2x8 — concrete piers

Two-thirds greenhouse and one-third storehouse, the shed *above* adapts to almost any family's gardening and storage requirements. Customize the unit with building materials to suit your own budget and site.

The 8x12-foot structure is built on a 4-inch concrete slab foundation with 2x4-inch studs and rafters (see the drawing *at right*). The greenhouse roof is covered with durable acrylic sheeting, and glass is used in the greenhouse walls. Texture 1-11 ⅝-inch plywood was used as siding. Rugged cedar shakes top the storage section, applied over ½-inch roof sheathing. For a finishing touch, we added 1-inch corner molding.

Inside, the plant benches and storage shelves are built with A-C grade plywood. All the plywood and interior lumber should be treated with

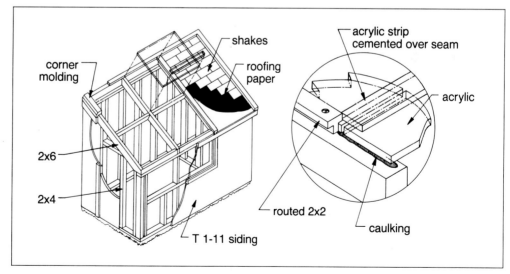

an effective wood preservative (one that won't harm the plants) to prevent the wood from rotting due to the high-humidity conditions of the greenhouse. All hardware should be brass, stainless

steel, or chrome, and all nails should be galvanized. Drip rails cut into the rafters help channel excess interior moisture away from the ceiling.

In cold climates, you'll want to add polystyrene foam insu-

lation between the studs, sealed by a polyethylene vapor barrier. You may also need a heating system suited to your plants and climate. Use tinted acrylic in the roof or add blinds if excess sunlight is a problem.

LIGHTING

Lights can shine brightly, glow softly, flood a whole patio, or highlight a special attraction. Outdoor lighting brings safety, security, and the opportunity to use your yard after dark. Here are some lighting ideas you might want to try, along with practical information about how to achieve them.

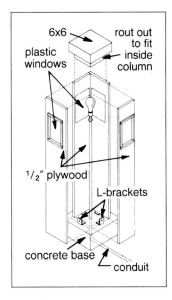

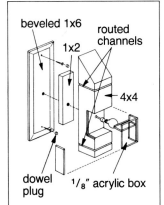

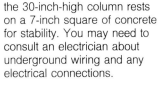

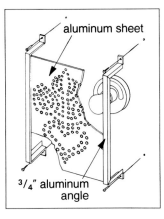

Well conceived and carefully placed, a handsome garden light like this one illuminates a path and adds a sculptural accent to your yard. Made of rough-sawn cedar plywood,

the 30-inch-high column rests on a 7-inch square of concrete for stability. You may need to consult an electrician about underground wiring and any electrical connections.

Highlight a patio, deck, or entry area at night with this handmade low-voltage light. Rough-sawn cedar or redwood forms the mount. Use a 12-volt marine or automotive light like the ones used for taillights or license plates. You'll also need a transformer to "step down" your household current. (See the box *opposite* for details on this procedure.) The bulb is covered with an acrylic box to keep out moisture.

You can eliminate glare from an outdoor light with a decorative light diffuser like the one shown here. Sandwich an aluminum sheet between hardboard and drill your design, or simply buy perforated metal. Make the sides by cutting notches in lengths of ¾-inch aluminum angle and bending them to

make U-shapes. Assemble the pieces with small galvanized bolts, drill holes in the ends of the angles, and screw the unit to the house. Be sure to allow space to change the bulb.

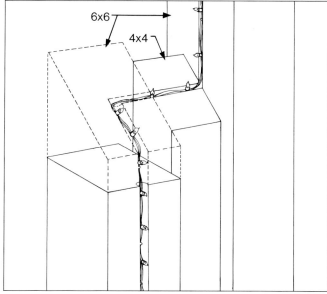

A graceful finishing touch dresses up this deck with a nighttime display of sparkling light. Low-voltage subminiature lamps strung on flexible ribbons outline the steps of the multilevel decking. Besides making a distinctive after-dark impression, the lights also contribute to safety. For a unified effect, mount matching lights in a routed groove on a post sculpture constructed of two 6x6s and one 4x4.

OUTDOOR WIRING

The basic principles that govern interior electrical work also apply to outdoor wiring, whether you're installing backyard lights or an outdoor receptacle. Because outdoor wiring is more vulnerable to moisture and physical damage, it does require a few extra precautions. For example, you should use either conduit with *Type-TW* wires pulled through it or *UF cable,* which is a tough and highly moisture-resistant sheathed cable. Check your local electrical code, since some specify one type in particular. Also check local restrictions about who can do the work and how it must be done.

If cable is used, you must protect it with conduit wherever the cable is aboveground. Underground cable should be buried at least 12 inches below the surface. Rigid conduit only needs to be 6 inches underground; thinner conduit must be 12 inches below the earth.

It's important to guard against serious shock by protecting outside circuits with a *ground-fault circuit interrupter* (GFCI)—a device that trips the circuit when even a tiny leakage occurs. Most codes require that all new 15- and 20-amp outdoor circuits use a GFCI for protection.

Running wires underground involves digging trenches, so you may want to rent a trencher. Begin by planning your routes, including where you want to penetrate the house wall.

Use a piece of rigid conduit to make the through-the-wall connection. Here you'll need an *LB* fitting as the exterior connector. It will help you make the sharp 90-degree turn downward. Run conduit from the fitting to the bottom of the trench and then at the other end from the bottom of the trench up to the receptacle or lamppost. Run the conduit or cable up the center of the lamppost, then set the post in a concrete pier with a sloped top.

Low-voltage wiring
Some outdoor wiring systems run on low voltages that are "stepped down" by a special transformer from 120-volt household currents to levels ranging from 6 to 30 volts. You can install these electrical subsystems without boxes, circuit breakers, fuses, or special grounding procedures.

Working with low-voltage circuits is ideal for do-it-yourselfers because the current is so low that the dangers of fire and shock are almost eliminated.

To install a new low-voltage device, start by running a circuit from the service panel to a conveniently located junction box. Then add a transformer and carry on from there with lightweight cable buried just a few inches below-ground or laid right on the surface. You can safely string together a series of fixtures like so many Christmas tree lights.

WHIRLIGIGS AND THINGAMAJIGS

It's the unpredictable that makes life—and yards—intriguing. So why not indulge your creative or mischievous impulses? A whirligig or thingamajig will delight you, the kids, and the local bird population. Here we show three whimsical touches that will please your family in any season—a bird feeder, birdhouse, and wind devices that are all inexpensive and fun to build. Place them where they can be seen from indoors for year-round enjoyment.

Mounted on the back fence, perched on the garage, or placed atop stakes in the yard, these wind "toys" promise to amuse and delight the young and the young-at-heart.

Each of the wind devices shown *opposite* puts on its own spinning, flashing show. The last four designs also indicate wind direction. Easy to assemble, any one of these devices can be built in an evening's time.

Use 18- and 20-gauge aluminum flashing and soft white pine scraps, plus wooden

beads and aluminum screws, nails, and washers to prevent rusting. Give all wood parts two coats of exterior varnish before assembling.

You can copy our designs or create one of your own, in the size and shape you prefer. Mount on ¾-inch posts.

For the birds
To build the birdhouse *above left*, use a 1-foot-long section of 4-inch clay drain tile, divided in the middle by a ¾-inch plywood plug. Wooden plugs with 1¾-inch holes for entry also form doorways. Two notched 2x6s hold the tile. Insert threaded rods above and below the tile and tighten the

nuts for a clamping effect. Before assembling the house, treat the 2x4s with preservative, paint, or stain.

A covered bird feeder like the one *above right* will attract lots of feathered friends to your yard. Make the 12x12-inch base from ⅛-inch hardboard. The side rails are 1x2s, butt-joined. Use aluminum for the 25x12-inch canopy. Drill four holes in each end of the roof and attach to the frame with wood screws.

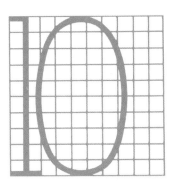

MAINTAINING YOUR YARD

Just as your yard at its best may be a miniature version of nature at her best, it also may present many of the same problems as nature at her less-than-best. The same forces that erode mountains and create rivers are at work on your patio, flower beds, walkways, and lawn. That's why, after winter freeze-ups and spring rains, you're likely to find the bricks in your patio separated, your concrete walks undermined and cracked, and your lawn bumpy. As you'll see in this chapter, routine maintenance can prevent a lot of these problems, and those that it can't, you can correct.

LAWN CARE

A rich, green, velvety lawn goes well with all kinds of houses and just about all types of plants. Even if you devote a major portion of your yard to other ground covers, or to a deck or patio, you're likely to have at least a handkerchief-size lawn to tend. And although some people spend hours caring for their lawns, the techniques of lawn care really aren't as complicated as some would have you believe. Just find the right type of turf for your climate and location, then set up a schedule to maintain it regularly.

The important thing to realize, as with any other kind of gardening, is that not all plants do well in all settings. *Cool-season grasses,* such as bluegrasses, fescues, and ryes, are suited for use in the North; *warm-season grasses,* such as Bermuda and St. Augustine grasses and the zoysias, do well in the South. For arid regions such as the Great Plains, there are special types, such as buffalo grass. A local garden center can advise you about grasses that grow well in your area.

If you're seeding, you'll find instructions for planting and initial care on the seed bags or boxes. Sodding and vegetative propagation (plugging, for example) are alternative methods for establishing grass in new lawns or sections of lawn. (See pages 34 and 35 for more about planting grasses.)

Once your lawn is established, you'll just be doing patchwork reseeding, sodding, or plugging. But that doesn't mean you're finished with lawn maintenance. An established lawn, if neglected, can quickly develop bare spots, sprout weeds, or become uneven.

Basic lawn maintenance
Several tasks need to be performed regularly if you want to keep your lawn looking good.
• During the growing season, mow your lawn regularly. Ideal heights vary by grass species, but many do best at about 2 inches. A good rule of thumb is to never cut off more than you leave, which means, in most cases, cutting the grass before or when it reaches 4 inches.
• Deep-water your lawn (to a depth of at least 6 inches) when it shows signs of drying out. Slowed growth, loss of resiliency, and a bluish or brown color are all signs that grass is in need of water.
• Fertilize your lawn once in the spring and again in the fall. Fertilizer usually is labeled by percentage of three nutrients—nitrogen, phosphorus, and potassium (always in that order). The fall fertilizer should have a 1-2-2 ratio; the desirable spring ratio is 2-1-1. Overfertilizing can make the grass turn brown and encourage top growth at the expense of a solid root system.

Special maintenance tasks
Sometimes, the most carefully tended lawn develops trouble spots. Repairs are easily made, but it's important to make them before the problem spreads or worsens.
• Bare spots have several causes; heavy foot traffic resulting in compacted soil is a common one. To repair bare spots, cultivate the soil to a depth of 4 to 6 inches and work fertilizer into the soil. Rake smooth, then sprinkle grass seed over the area. Tamp the seed into the soil surface. Cover the bare spot with sterile, weed-free straw or burlap; water lightly and regularly until new growth is established.
• If your lawn appears to be lumpy and contains low spots,

wait until you're well into spring to do something about it. Otherwise, you may be correcting a frost-heaving problem that would have resettled and solved itself. To fix permanent low spots, simply fill them with a weed-free topsoil. Water to help settle the new material, then repeat the process until the low spot disappears. Seed as described above. If your lawn is sodded, temporarily roll back the strips, fill underneath with topsoil, and return the strips to their original positions. For high spots and small mounds caused by night crawlers and moles, use a heavy roller to flatten the ground.

• Thatch, a decaying leaf and root matter, is useful up to a point, because it serves as fertilizer and controls weed growth. But if allowed to build up, thatch can strangle your lawn by preventing new growth and providing a home for insects and disease. Remove thatch with a sturdy rake or a specially made dethatching power rake, then fertilize and reseed your lawn.

• Weeds and pests are a part of any gardener's domain. If damage has reached unacceptable levels, use pesticides and herbicides as needed to rid your lawn of blights and weeds. A convenient option is to use a "weed and feed" product, which combines two operations in one. Make sure you use them only on lawns where grass is established, because pesticides and herbicides can slow the growth of new seed. Keep in mind also that some substances are potentially hazardous to children, animals, and other plants; don't apply chemicals on a windy day.

For more information about lawn care and seasonal tasks, see the chart *at right*.

SEASONAL LAWN CARE

EARLY SPRING

Cool-season grasses: *March* may feel like spring, but the weather is too changeable for you to start any real lawn work. Clean your lawn mower and have it sharpened, if this wasn't done at the end of the previous growing season. When soil has dried enough so you can walk on the lawn without leaving footprints, probably in *April,* clear debris and branches that have accumulated over the winter. Rake grass that has been matted down by snow; you may have to dethatch if you didn't do this last fall. Seed bare spots that were neglected during the prime fall planting season. Apply preemergent weed control agents for crabgrass and other annual weeds. Apply fertilizer in late *April* or early *May.* Also in *May,* lay sod if necessary.
Warm-season grasses: Starting in late *March* and going into *April,* aerate for better penetration of air, water, and fertilizer. Dethatch two to three weeks after your lawn turns green. Sow seed when soil has warmed thoroughly. Fertilize as necessary for your grass type. Apply preemergent weed control agents for crabgrass and other annual weeds.

LATE SPRING/ MID- SUMMER

Cool-season grasses: Level the bumps and hollows in your lawn to minimize mowing problems. Grass will grow vigorously from *May* to *July;* mow at least once a week. Identify any weeds sprouting and apply appropriate weed killer one to two weeks after fertilizing. Check for pests; identify them and get an appropriate pesticide. As rainfall lessens and growth slows, start watering and mow less often; taller grasses withstand heat better and can shade crabgrass and other sun-loving weeds. Don't apply any chemicals in extreme heat. Fertilizers and pesticides shock grass whenever they're applied, and in hot, dry weather grasses don't have the stamina to withstand the extra stress.
Warm-season grasses: Plant sprigs or stolons of some varieties; sod-laying season starts now, too. Reapply fertilizer. As weather gets warmer, keep watering at the rate of about 1 inch a week. Mow more frequently as growth rate increases.

LATE SUMMER/ FALL

Cool-season grasses: *August* is a good time to start new lawns or overseed patchy ones in the coolest sections of the country; elsewhere, wait until *September.* Fertilize. Mow more often as the grass resumes a faster growing rate. Avoid overwatering, but do water heavily right before the ground freezes. Starting in *October,* rake fallen leaves. At end of season, clean and sharpen the mower so you won't have to do it next March.
Warm-season grasses: Apply insecticides and pesticides and continue mowing and watering as necessary. Make the last application of fertilizer before grass goes dormant. Overseeding can start now and continue until *December,* depending on climate. Aerate before overseeding. Keep seedbed moist to ensure rapid growth.

CARING FOR TREES AND SHRUBS

Many yard maintenance tasks—pruning, mulching, even watering—prepare plants for harsh weather, protect them from it when it comes, and repair any damage caused by the weather. Precise schedules and requirements vary by region and age and type of plant, of course, but on the next few pages you'll find a run-down of the hows and whys of some of the most basic chores.

Whether you have a thickly growing hedge of evergreens or just a couple of flowering ornamentals, you've probably noticed how quickly trees and shrubs can grow out of bounds or lose their graceful shapes if they're not properly pruned.

Pruning is a safety measure, too. If you notice a branch—or tree—that seems to have the potential to fall on people or property, cut the branch before the accident occurs. And keep an eye on older trees to make sure they have no open wounds, fungi, dead bark, or broken, jagged branches—all are indications that wood-weakening insects or diseases may have invaded the tree.

Beyond the general categories of good looks and preventive maintenance, there are specific reasons to prune trees and shrubs. Here are some of the most important.
• To remove dead, broken, or diseased branches.
• To accentuate natural shapes or reshape for special purposes, such as screening an undesirable view or opening up an attractive one.
• To renew old plants and encourage new growth.
• To eliminate suckers and unwanted new growth.
• To limit size.
• To produce new fall growth for winter color.
• To help plants withstand the shock of transplanting by compensating for root loss.

The best time to prune is late winter or early spring, when the first burst of spring growth will help the cuts heal quickly. In addition, deciduous trees and shrubs have no leaves at this time, making it easier to discern the shape of the branches. (Prune spring-flowering shrubs right after the blossoms have faded.)

Here are a few basic principles to consider before you start pruning.
• Heavy pruning on top of shrubs—not trees—encourages leaves and branches to grow; pruning roots prior to transplanting increases flower and fruit production and decreases leaf production. Again, don't do this to trees.
• Cutting back terminal buds, those that grow at the tips of branches, forces lateral, or side, buds to develop, resulting in a bushier plant.
• Established young trees need as many of their leaves as possible to make food used for growing, so cut off no more than one or two lower branches each year, no matter what shape you want the tree to take. But newly planted bare root stock could need as much as two-thirds of its branches removed.

Shrubs often can tolerate more drastic cutting back than trees. Removing about 10 or 12 inches of top growth from the crown and sides of many shrubs each year will stimulate side-branching, resulting in a more compact plant. You can—and should—annually cut back a few old branches to the ground on some shrubs, such as forsythia and honeysuckle.

Although pruning is a subtle art, you only need three basic tools to do the job: a pruning shears for light trimming, a saw for larger branches, and a long-handled lopper for reaching high sprouts and thick twigs. Check with your local garden center or extension agent for specific pruning advice. Leave major tree surgery to professionals.

Mulching and wrapping

Young trees, shrubs, and many perennials benefit from mulching to reduce moisture loss, protect roots from.

extreme temperatures, and, in the case of smaller plants, keep weed growth to a minimum. In most cases, mulch should be applied in late spring or early summer, when soil is warm and dry enough to be workable. Pine bark, well-decayed manure, leaf mold, peat moss, ground corncobs, grass clippings, and semi-decayed wood chips are all popular—availability is often regional, and some types may be more suitable for certain soil grades and plants.

A layer of mulch 2 to 3 inches thick is sufficient for a young tree and shrubs. Be sure to leave an uncovered circle of at least 2 inches around the base. This reduces the threat of both rodent damage and decay from excessive moisture retention.

Wrapping, another protective device, is especially important for young, recently planted trees and shrubs. Use special paper, burlap, or aluminum foil to protect the plantings from strong sun, wind, rodents and rabbits, insect borers, and lawn-mower nicks.

Even mature shrubs and trees of some types—notably broadleaf evergreens such as rhododendrons and needle-leaf evergreens such as pine and juniper—require rigorous protection in winter. Add mulch around their bases to achieve a total depth of 3 to 6 inches. The cold winds of winter are especially drying to evergreens, which lose moisture through their leaves yet are unable to obtain it through their roots from the frozen ground. In late fall and again in January or February, you can apply an antidesiccant spray that forms a protective film on the leaves. Deep-watering before the ground freezes also can help prevent dangerous drying, and another soaking in February, is a good idea. If your plants are especially exposed to wind, you can shield them with a burlap or wood windbreak.

Watering

As noted before, deep-watering is the key to proper lawn watering. With some exceptions, a similar rule applies to trees and shrubs.

• *Newly planted trees* need watering every two weeks and every week in hot, dry weather. Don't turn off the hose until the water stops seeping quickly into the ground. Once the leaves drop off deciduous trees in autumn, stop regular watering, then give trees, particularly evergreens, one more thorough soaking before the ground freezes for the winter (unless it's been a very wet fall and the ground is already saturated).

• *Fully established, mature trees* don't need regular watering unless the weather is extremely hot and dry for a prolonged period. Their root systems are deep and complex enough to reach water under most conditions.

• *Newly planted shrubs* also need careful watering. Leave a shallow depression around them and soak the area. Water deeply again after a few days. In contrast with most transplanted trees, newly planted shrubs are not necessarily young ones. Many mature shrubs can be moved safely, especially during the summer months. In addition to deep-watering them after planting, cool newly transplanted shrubs in hot weather by lightly misting them with a garden hose. Avoid overwatering. Once a week is enough for subsequent deep-watering, except when it's very hot and dry, when you may have to water as often as every day.

SOME FACTORS TO CONSIDER BEFORE PLANTING

As you choose the trees and plants that will best complement your yard and thrive in the miniclimate you'll be providing, consider the effects the plants will have on you and your environment. For example, some plants with appealing foliage, flowers, or berries attract colorful birds. Others are especially fragrant. If you have young children or free-roaming pets, you may want to avoid poisonous plants that could present a hazard to innocent nibblers.

The following are lists—by no means all-inclusive—of plants in these special categories. Your county extension service or garden center can provide information about the landscaping materials that are best suited to your area.

Attracting birds

Shrubs and trees that provide nesting sites and bright berries are among the best candidates for bird-lovers' yards. Here are just a few.
Arrowwood (shrub)
Japanese barberry (shrub)
Bayberry (shrub)
Boxwood (shrub)
Crabapple (tree)
Virginia creeper (vine)
Dogwood (tree)
American elder (tree)
Hawthorn (shrub)
Honeysuckle (vine)
Mulberry (shrub)

Flowering quince (tree)
Serviceberry (tree)
Snowberry (shrub)
Sweet gum (tree)
Winterberry (shrub)

Fragrance

Fragrance is one of the great pleasures of outdoor living, and a sweet-smelling herb garden or shrubbery hedge can be a delight. Here are some varieties of herbs, perennials, vines, shrubs, and other plants to consider when planning a fragrant garden.
Swamp azalea (shrub)
Sweet alyssum (annual)
Candytuft (annual)
Chamomile (herb)
Dianthus (perennial)
Four-o'clock (annual)
Freesia (bulb)
Heliotrope (annual)
Honeysuckle (vine)
Lavender (herb)
Lilac (shrub)
Auratum lily (bulb)
Regal lily (bulb)
Lily-of-the-valley (perennial)
Nicotiana (annual)
Mock orange (shrub)
Rose (shrub)
Stock (annual)
Sweet pea (annual)
Flowering witch hazel (shrub)

Poisonous plants

Many poisonous plants, such as pokeberry and baneberry, are weeds; others, unfortunately, are beautiful and desirable. Contact-poison plants such as poison ivy, poison sumac, and stinging nettles are quite well known and often recog-

nized—and rarely find their way into well-tended gardens. But many popular landscaping plants (or parts of them) are poisonous if ingested. Here is a brief list of some of the most common toxic plants. The plant parts that are poisonous are listed in parentheses. If your household includes children or pets who are likely to consume parts of plants, you might want to avoid planting these, or at least make sure you place them where they won't be accessible to unwary residents or passersby. If you have questions about plants in your yard or house, check with the local extension service or the poison control center *before* a leaf or berry is eaten.
Wild black cherry (foliage)
Bleeding-heart (roots and stem)
Caladium (all parts)
Castor bean plant (seeds)
Autumn crocus (roots and stem)
Daphne (all parts)
Delphinium (foliage)
Foxglove (foliage)
Golden chain (seeds)
Carolina jasmine (juice)
Annual lantana (berries)
Laurels (foliage)
Lily-of-the-valley (roots and stems)
Mayapple, or mandrake (roots and fruit)
Oleander (all parts)
Poinsettia (juice)
Rhododendron (foliage)
Rhubarb (leaves)
Christmas rose (juice)
Wisteria (seeds)

PEST CONTROL

As much as you may enjoy nature and feel a kinship with living things, it's hard to hold on to your warm feelings when hordes of blood-sucking mosquitoes attack you, or voracious rabbits devour your lettuces. Before you declare war on all winged and four-legged creatures that trespass on your outdoor hospitality, stop to consider that some actually may be worth cultivating. On this page we'll tell you about them. The chart on the next page tells how to control unwanted wildlife.

You may not like spiders and toads, but they are among your foremost garden allies when it comes to controlling insects. Along with birds and a variety of other small creatures, spiders and toads consume biting, plant-eating pests in amazing numbers. Here's a rundown of some species you should know about.

Insects that eat insects

The *ladybug*, probably the best-known garden benefactor, is actually a beetle, and more properly known as a *ladybird*. The most common variety has 12 or 13 black spots on its reddish back. Both adult ladybugs and larvae, or juvenile bugs, eat soft-bodied insects such as aphids, mealybugs, leafhoppers, scale insects, and the eggs and larvae of these and other small pests. One ladybug eats 50 aphids a day.

Less colorful but more dramatic in shape—and with an equally insatiable appetite—is the *praying mantis,* named for the way the mantis stands poised to grab unsuspecting aphids, caterpillars, grasshoppers, and other insects.

You can order both praying mantis egg cases and ladybugs by mail from nurseries around the country. A quart of hungry ladybugs should be enough for a large yard. A mantis egg case contains more than 200 eggs, which will hatch when the weather is warm enough to bring out the native insects that make up the entire diet of the patient but hungry mantis fledglings.

Lacewings are called *aphid lions* because of their fondness for aphids. They'll also eat mealybugs, mites, and thrips.

Ground, or *carabid, beetles* hide under boards and stones and thrive on caterpillars, slugs, and other insects.

Syrphid flies are quite often mistaken for bees; the bright yellow-and-black adults do, in fact, help with pollination. Syrphid fly larvae look like slugs, but one larva can destroy an aphid in a minute.

Remember chasing *fireflies,* or *lightning bugs* when you were small? These flying light shows are really beetles whose favorite feasts include cutworms, snails, and slugs.

The exotic-looking *dragonfly* and its delicate-seeming cousin, the *damselfly,* originated the concept of in-flight meals. One of their favorite snacks is the dreaded mosquito.

Parasite insects

The tiny *trichogramma wasp* lays its minute eggs inside the eggs of some 200 species of harmful pests, including tomato and cabbage worms and fruit moths. The wasp larvae then destroy the host eggs. Trichogramma wasps are available by mail.

The *braconid wasp* zeroes in on aphids and the larvae of many beetles and moths, including tent caterpillars and cutworms. The white, egg-shaped cocoons you see attached to a tomato hornworm are often the pupae of wasps that went through the larval stage inside the worm's body.

Other helpful insect parasites include the *polistes wasp,* which attacks tobacco hornworm, corn earworm, and armyworm; *ichneumon fly,* which helps control tomato worms and fruit moths; and *tachinid fly,* which preys on caterpillars, Japanese beetles, moths, squash bugs, tomato worms, and grasshoppers.

Other garden allies

The diet of *spiders* consists mostly of insects. The golden orb spider, for example, helps eradicate Japanese beetles from raspberry bushes. And, the brown wood spider that nests in garden mulch has an insatiable appetite for grasshoppers.

The friendly *wren* prefers leafhoppers, plant lice, scale insects, whiteflies, and even the tiniest insect eggs. Put up a wren house to encourage a pair to settle in your yard.

The food preferences of the *titmouse* and the *bushtit* are similar to those of the wren. *Purple martins* and other swallows scoop up flies, wasps, and other bugs on the wing. Keep a birdbath filled with regularly freshened water to attract birds.

Toads, even though they're not princes in disguise as promised by the fairy tale, have a welcome place in the garden. During the night, they eat just about any small thing that moves, especially cutworms, slugs, and potato beetles. One toad devours up to 15,000 insects annually. Provide a shallow container of water to encourage toads to remain in your garden.

Pesticides

When you have to resort to pesticides, be careful to use the proper mixture for the specific problem you're dealing with. Follow the label directions and resist the impulse to use more than is recommended.

Keep in mind that many of the problems attributed to insects or diseases are not caused by them at all. Yellowing, discoloration, wilting, stunting, and curling or deformation of the plant foliage may also be symptoms of other common problems, such as nutritional deficiency, toxic chemicals (air pollution, other pesticides, salts, or too much fertilizer), lack of or too much water, not enough or too much sunlight, or winter damage.

UNWELCOME VISTORS

Rabbits. Peter Cottontail and his brethren are public enemy number one of backyard crops and landscape plants. During the winter, rabbits can be captured easily in covered box-traps (wooden or wire boxes covered with cloth) and removed to the edge of town or to a wildlife preserve. To protect shrubs and trees during the dormant season, paint the trunks and lower branches with one of several chemical repellents. Most of these are based on thiram, a fungicide. A cylinder of ¼-inch wire mesh, or hardware cloth, wrapped around a tree trunk provides excellent protection. Be sure that the cloth extends well above the depth of expected snowfall.

For spring garden protection, a low fence is effective. It need not be more than 18 inches high or more than a few inches into the soil, but be sure the mesh opening is no larger than 1 inch, or young rabbits will go right through it.

Raccoons. Raccoons raid garbage cans, devastate garden patches, and take up residence in attics, crawl spaces, or chimneys. The best way to deal with raccoons is to capture them in a large, sturdy live-trap and then relocate them to a suitable wooded area. Sardines, catfood, and fish or meat scraps make effective bait.

Bats. Even though bats eat insects, they are not popular with humans. To keep them out of your house, seal all cracks or holes larger than ⅜ inch. Bats do not gnaw at closed openings as squirrels and rats do. Make sure that you close openings after dark, when the bats are out feeding, or in late fall (in northern states), when they have left for winter quarters.

Moles. The distinctive ridges that suddenly appear on lawns are the feeding tunnels of moles. Your garden center can suggest an insecticide to control the insect grubs that moles feed on. A more direct and effective approach is to trap the moles. Several types of specialized mole traps are available.

Squirrels and gophers. Tree squirrels, ground squirrels (as chipmunks are sometimes called), and gophers do a lot of excavating, which can damage seeds, bulbs, and tree roots. Tree (gray and fox) squirrels raid bird feeders and nest in attics. The best way to remove tree squirrels from an attic is to use a box-trap or cover their entrance hole with wire mesh. To ward off ground squirrels, buy a rodenticide and place it in their burrows. Or try flooding the ground squirrels out of their burrows with a garden hose. Special traps combat gophers.

Deer. Discourage hungry deer from feeding on your tree bark and garden with 6- to 8-foot fencing and any of a wide range of commercial repellents based on such substances as thiram, putrified eggs, hot pepper sauce, and bone tar oil. Small mesh bags of human hair, mothballs, and blood meal may also provide relief.

Birds. The three major bird pests are pigeons, starlings, and house sparrows. The last two are particularly troublesome because of their aggressive nesting behavior. Sparrows, for example, may overrun a purple martin house. To discourage these pests, remove their nests with a hooked wire as soon as the nests appear.

Robins and other birds with a fondness for fruit can make life miserable for a gardener trying to raise cherries, blueberries, or strawberries. Cover the entire tree or berry patch with bird-proof netting just before the fruit is ripe. Many types of netting are available; the plastic ones are inexpensive and will last for many seasons.

Woodpeckers pose a serious problem by drumming holes through your siding. The drumming may be associated with territorial behavior or a search for insects. Overwintering insects and insect larvae are often harbored in the tunnels of certain types of plywood. If insects are the attraction, try to caulk all openings to these tunnels. Using a wood preservative or insecticide may help. If insects do not seem to be present, you'll have to resort to scaring the birds away. For example, use foil strips, windmill-type toys, rubber snakes, or hawk or owl decoys.

Gypsy moths. A single caterpillar can devour up to seven leaves a day. Biologically based *Bacillus thuringiensis,* often called BT, will kill the caterpillars without harming the gypsy moth's natural enemies, such as birds and small wasps. Chemical controls include acephate (Orthene), methoxychlor, and imidan. Traps containing a strong sex lure will attract and kill many male moths. You can attach a barrier tape to tree trunks to foil the caterpillars.

Japanese beetles. Not a finicky eater, this beetle eats as many as 275 forms of flowers, foliage, fruits, and vegetables. Milky spore bacteria placed on lawns and other grassy areas help combat Japanese beetles. Or buy a trap containing a floral lure plus a synthesized sex attractant that emits the scent of 80,000 virgin Japanese beetles. This irresistible bait draws Japanese beetles from as far away as 100 yards. The trap contains no toxic substances, so there's no ground or air pollution.

Mosquitoes. These vampires of the insect world go looking for blood mainly in the evening, when you're most likely to be relaxing outside. You may want to apply an insect repellent to your skin before you venture out. Purple martins consume vast quantities of mosquitoes, so you might think of installing an apartment house for martins. And don't forget to search for and eliminate mosquitoes' favorite breeding ground: areas of stagnant water.

FENCE, GATE, AND DECK REPAIRS

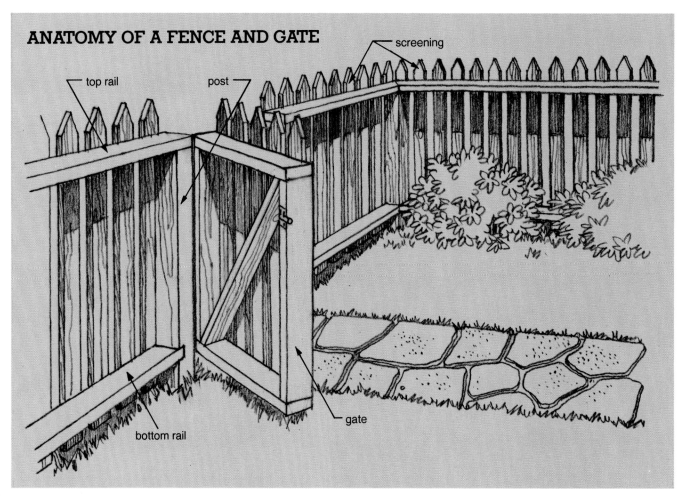

ANATOMY OF A FENCE AND GATE

screening

top rail

post

bottom rail

gate

Most fences are made of vertical *posts,* horizontal *rails,* often some sort of *screening* suspended on the rails, and *gates.* If they are not made from redwood, cypress, or pressure-treated wood, all parts should be adequately protected against insects and rot with preservatives or paint. Ungalvanized metal fences should be protected against rust by priming and painting.

Fixing fences

If some parts of your fence suffer from excessive rot or corrosion, replace them. Otherwise, target your efforts just on the problem areas by scraping, sanding, or wire-brushing away the rot or corrosion, filling any holes, and then spot-preserving and/or painting.

If frost heaving has caused your fence posts to stand awry, straighten them by driving preserved wooden wedges into the ground around the base, using a level on any two adjoining sides of the posts to check for plumb. To ensure that the posts remain upright, widen the postholes and deepen them to below the frost line. Clean the posts and reset them in concrete, beveling the concrete at ground level away from the post for proper drainage. (You may need new posts to achieve the desired height.)

With broken rail or screening members, fasten the broken pieces back together again using a waterproof adhesive and nails or screws. If this doesn't work, replace the rail or screening member.

Gates

If gates sag, check to see that the hinges are firmly secured to the support post and gate. If not, remove the screws, insert toothpicks or wood splinters into the screw holes, then reattach the hardware. Tighten loose latch hardware while you're at it.

If sagging persists, check the gate posts for plumb, correcting them if needed. Should these measures fail, check the gate for square. Gate frame members could have worked apart and may need regluing and clamping. Maintain a wooden gate's shape by screwing on metal angle plates at the corners or by placing a 1x4 diagonal between opposing corners. To learn more about fences and gates, see pages 88-91.

Good fences really do make good neighbors—and they can do a lot for the appearance of your yard, too. If your fences, gates, or decks need mending, read on.

ANATOMY OF A DECK

rail

screening

beam

post

pier

decking

joist

tread

stringer

Despite the fact that deck members are typically cedar, redwood, pressure-treated wood, or painted wood, all of which offer some protection against the elements and pests, even the best-built decks cannot escape the effects of weathering.

Regular maintenance
To preserve your deck, it's important to maintain it on a regular basis. Do this by scrubbing away collected dirt and by scraping and sanding all areas where paint is peeling. Then recoat the deck with a sealer, preservative, stain, or paint, as desired. When doing so, drive in any popped nails and tighten any loose lag screws or bolts with a wrench.

During rains or when snow melts on a deck, water penetrates the wood, especially at board ends and joints where it can cause rot. *Posts, beams,* and *joists* are particularly prone to rot, because they're often near ground level and covered by decking. Over time this usually means replacing weak, spongy members with strong new members of the same size and wood type.

Mildew is another moisture-related problem. To combat mildew, scrub the affected area with a mixture of water and household bleach, or use a mildewcide.

In addition to water, wear takes its toll on *deck rails* and *stair treads* and *stringers*. If any of these members feel spongy, or if gaping cracks appear along their lengths, replace them immediately.

Structural strategy
Don't tear down the entire deck if it rests at an angle; a salvageable deck may only need replacement of posts that are bowed, rotted at the base, or settled. Provide new support posts that stand on solid concrete piers that extend below the frost line. Be sure the deck has a slight slope (¼ inch per foot) away from the house for proper drainage. For more about deck construction, see pages 82-87.

CARING FOR OUTDOOR SURFACES AND ACCESSORIES

Outdoor surfaces and equipment have to be tough to withstand temperature extremes, exposure to the elements, and heavy use season after season. Even the most durable surfaces and equipment, however, periodically need some preventive or corrective maintenance. The chart *at right* identifies the kinds of damage that different yard surfaces are vulnerable to and how to repair them. *Opposite,* you'll find information about keeping outdoor accessories and equipment at their best.

MAINTAINING YARD SURFACES

WOOD	Treat any portion of wood touching or below ground with a preservative to resist rot and insects. (Exceptions are cedar, redwood, cypress, and pressure-treated lumbers that contain natural or manufactured preservatives.) Common preservatives include creosote, pentachlorophenol, and copper naphthenate. Seal aboveground wood with a preservative or an exterior paint or stain. Here, too, cedar, redwood, and cypress can be left to weather naturally.
STONE FLAGGING	Flagging embedded in mortar sometimes can pop loose or break in two. Or the mortar surrounding the flagging can crack and work out of the joint. Correct these problems by removing the loose flagging and/or mortar. Chisel and wire-brush all the surfaces until clean and smooth. Then moisten the cavity and apply new mortar, re-laying the same stone (if it's ok) or using a new custom-cut stone. Finish by striking the joints. To protect against stains, apply a sealer over the flagging. Immediately wipe up all spills and scrub with a detergent and water solution if necessary.
CONCRETE AND EXPOSED AGGREGATE	For minor flaws like spalling (or flaking) and fine cracks, use a latex, vinyl, or epoxy patch material. Also use epoxy adhesive to reinsert loosened stones in an aggregate surface. To repair large damaged areas, remove the old broken concrete pieces, build a form, and pour in premixed concrete. Sop up fresh oil and grease stains with sawdust. For paint, use an appropriate solvent; for rust, try rubbing bleach on the stain.
BRICK	Moisture can freeze and expand in sand or mortared joints, causing brick patios to literally come apart at the seams. With sand joints, remove the bricks, level the sand bedding (adding new sand if necessary), and reinstall the bricks and joints. With mortared joints, remove all loose material, clean the cavities with a chisel and wire brush, and remortar the bricks and/or joints. This same procedure applies when tuck-pointing brick walls. To remove efflorescence from brick, scrub the area with a 1:10 solution of muriatic acid and water. Be sure to wear protective clothing and use a long-handled brush.
ASPHALT	Fill small cracks partway with sand, then top them off with asphalt crack filler. For potholes, tamp in asphalt cold patch. Large-scale repairs require resurfacing by a professional asphalt company.
GRAVEL	Gravel has a tendency to spread out; maintain it by raking the gravel back into place and, if you desire, adding wood or stone borders. If gravel has compacted and worked into the soil, you may need to add new material to maintain the original level.

Yard equipment and accessories that have been cleaned, maintained, and stored properly at the end of their "active" season will be ready and waiting to serve you next year.

Give lawn furniture and portable barbecue grills a thorough scouring before storing indoors. Check outdoor furniture for rust or nicks in paint; remove rust, then prime and spot-repaint.

Seal opened packages of lawn and garden chemicals, and store them in a dry place out of children's reach.

Tool care

With a scraper, remove all encrusted dirt from rakes, shovels, hoes, and other tools. Get rid of rust with aluminum oxide sandpaper or a wire brush, then sharpen and oil your tools. Hang tools for storage rather than leaving them in contact with cold, damp floors in a shed or garage.

If you own a sprayer, duster, or lawn spreader, hose it out, paying particular attention to nozzles and other parts that clog up.

Prepare your lawn mower for winter storage by thoroughly cleaning its housing and underside. Drain oil and gas from the tank and gas line; gas left standing for several months will evaporate and leave gummy deposits. Fill with new oil and remove the spark plug. Have blades sharpened; coat them with a thin layer of oil for protection. In the spring, fill the gas tank, install a new spark plug, and you'll be ready to mow.

The chart *at right* outlines problems that can arise with outdoor accessories and steps to take to correct them.

MAINTAINING ACCESSORIES

PROBLEMS	SOLUTIONS

EXTERIOR FAUCETS

Pipes leading to a faucet freeze and burst. A leaking faucet soaks the foundation wall and causes water damage within.	To prevent pipes from freezing, drain them in the fall and leave the faucet open, install a freezeproof faucet, or wrap the pipes with electric heat tape. Fix faucet leaks by replacing worn washers.

HOSES

Hoses lying around on the lawn can be accidentally chopped up during the mowing season; hoses left out past frost will freeze and crack. Leaks at nozzles, couplings, or along the hose itself cause a drop in hose pressure.	Drain and store hoses when not in use. Store on an outside reel, or in a figure-eight pattern on the floor indoors. When temperatures drop below freezing, bring all hoses indoors. Immediately repair hose leaks to maintain maximum hose pressure. Replace faulty washers, nozzles, and couplings; cut out sections of bad hose and rejoin with a mending kit.

SCREENS AND STORM WINDOWS

Peeling paint, dirt, missing glazing compound, torn screening, and broken glass lead to more severe deterioration if neglected. Also, loose frames result in a bad fit.	Make repairs during the off-seasons: spring and summer for storms and fall and winter for screens. After removing them from window openings, hose off screens and wash storms. Mend torn screens and replace broken glass. Rejoin loose frames and refinish old surfaces; scrape off deteriorated glazing compound, prime the frame with linseed oil, and apply new compound. Clean aluminum frames with car polish.

GUTTERS AND DOWNSPOUTS

Flaking paint, accumulated debris, corrosion, and loosened hardware keep roof drainage systems from doing their jobs.	In autumn, after the leaves have fallen, hose out leaf deposits and silt from your drainage system. Refinish the system with primer and paint, if needed, and refasten all loose hardware.

COMPRESSORS

Accumulated dirt and debris clog the protective grill on the outside of the unit and reduce airflow. Dirty coils further reduce efficiency. A squeaky blower fan is a nuisance.	In spring, hose out debris from the compressor unit. Remove the housing and vacuum dirt from condenser fins and coils. Oil the fan motor. Make sure power is off when doing any work on a compressor.

WHERE TO GO FOR MORE INFORMATION

Better Homes and Gardens® Books
Would you like to learn more about planning and maintaining
your yard? These Better Homes and Gardens® books can help.

Better Homes and Gardens®
COMPLETE GUIDE TO GARDENING
A comprehensive guide for beginners and experienced
gardeners. Houseplants, lawns and landscaping, trees and
shrubs, greenhouses, and insects and diseases. 461 color
photos, 434 how-to illustrations, 37 charts, 552 pages.

Better Homes and Gardens®
COMPLETE GUIDE TO HOME REPAIR,
MAINTENANCE & IMPROVEMENT
Inside your home, outside your home, your home's systems,
basics you should know. Anatomy and step-by-step drawings
illustrate components, tools, techniques, and finishes.
515 how-to techniques, 75 charts, 2,734 illustrations, 552 pages.

Better Homes and Gardens®
STEP-BY-STEP
BASIC PLUMBING
Getting to know your system, solving plumbing problems, making
plumbing improvements, and plumbing basics and procedures.
42 projects, 200 illustrations, 96 pages.

Better Homes and Gardens®
STEP-BY-STEP
BASIC WIRING
Getting to know your system, solving electrical problems, making
electrical improvements, and electrical basics and procedures.
22 projects, 286 illustrations, 96 pages.

Better Homes and Gardens®
STEP-BY-STEP
BASIC CARPENTRY
Setting up shop, choosing tools and building materials, mastering
construction techniques, building boxes, hanging shelves,
framing walls, and installing drywall and paneling. 10 projects,
191 illustrations, 96 pages.

Better Homes and Gardens®
STEP-BY-STEP
MASONRY & CONCRETE
Choosing tools and materials; planning masonry projects;
working with concrete; working with brick, block, and stone; and
special-effect projects. 10 projects, 200 drawings, 96 pages.

Better Homes and Gardens®
STEP-BY-STEP
HOUSEHOLD REPAIRS
Basic tools for repair jobs; repairing walls and ceilings, floors and
stairs, windows and doors, and electrical and plumbing items.
200 illustrations, 96 pages.

Better Homes and Gardens®
STEP-BY-STEP
CABINETS & SHELVES
Materials and hardware, planning guidelines, the ABCs of cabinet
construction, cutting and joining techniques, project potpourri.
155 illustrations, 96 pages.

Other Sources of Information
Most professional associations publish lists of their members,
and will be happy to furnish these lists upon request. They also
may offer educational material and other information.

California Redwood Association
591 Redwood Highway
Suite 3100
Mill Valley, CA 94941

Western Wood Products Association
1500 Yeon Building
Portland, OR 97204

American Plywood Association
7011 S. 19th Street
P.O. Box 11700
Tacoma, WA 98411

National Spa and Pool Institute
2000 K Street, NW
Washington, DC 20006

ACKNOWLEDGMENTS

Architects and Designers

The following is a page-by-page listing of the architects and designers whose work appears in this book.

Pages 6-7
Michael K. Bartlett, A.I.A.
Pages 8-9
Peter Dejana
Pages 10-11
Peter Golze
Pages 12-13
Galper/Baldon Associates; Richard K. O'Grady; design sponsor: California Redwood Association
Pages 14-15
Walt Young
Pages 18-19
Joe Eigner
Pages 20-21
Gene Fox
Pages 22-23
Roger Macon and Ivanka Peke
Pages 24-25
Allan W. Hall, A.I.A.
Pages 30-31
Thomas Scott Dean, A.I.A.
Pages 32-33
Burnett and Garrett
Pages 40-41
Robert Aiken; Decks Unlimited
Pages 42-43
Atlantic Nurseries
Pages 44-45
Scherer & Sons
Pages 46-47
Steve Adams; Ireland/Viette Nursery Landscaping
Pages 48-49
Barbara Cunningham; Don Morria; Jack Smith
Pages 52-53
Agnes Bourne; Wilkes and Faulkner; Atlantic Nurseries; J. Matthias; design sponsor: California Redwood Association
Pages 56-57
Joseph Copp, Jr.

Pages 60-61
Jack Woodson; Robert J. Clark; Nan Warren
Pages 76-77
Stephen Mead Associates
Pages 110-111
Goldberg/Rodler
Pages 112-113
Howard and Janie Atkinson; Elena Binckley Blauvelt, A.S.I.D.
Pages 114-115
Leo E. Schuster
Pages 116-117
Richard Bishop; Sabin, O'Neal, Mitchell, A.I.A.
Pages 118-119
Fran Lechtrecker
Pages 122-123
Gerry Mac Cartee
Pages 124-125
Pacific Aquaculture
Pages 128-129
Peter and Sylvia Chan; Alfred Drumright
Pages 130-131
Margaret O'Neil
Pages 132-133
Alice and Cliff Grant
Pages 136-137
Michael Walsh and Morris McKnight
Pages 138-139
Bryan McCay; Garth Graves
Pages 140-141
Design sponsor: American Plywood Association; David Carmen
Pages 142-143
Donald H. Benson; Jim Laing, Wood Butcher Hot Tubs; David Ashe
Pages 144-145
David Ashe

Photographers and Illustrators

We extend our thanks to the following photographers and illustrators whose creative talents and technical skills contributed much to this book.
Mike Blaser
Ernest Braun
Ross Chapple
Jim Cobb

George de Gennaro
Mike Dieter
Harry Hartman
Hedrich/Blessing
Bill Helms
Hopkins Associates
Scott Little
Fred Lyon
Maris/Semel
E. Alan McGee
Jordan Miller
John Rogers
Jim Stevenson
Sandra Williams

Associations and Companies

Our appreciation goes to the following associations and companies for providing information and materials for this book.

Alcan
American Plywood Association
Arkla Industries
A. Brandt
Brown Jordan
California Redwood Association
Coleman Patio Products Co., Inc.
Des Moines Seed and Nursery
Drip Mist
Gardener's Eden
Gold Medal, Inc.
Howmet Aluminum Corporation
I.C.F.
Little Giant Pump Company
Melnor Industries
Pawley's Island Hammock Co.
Pestolite, Inc.
Rain Bird
Rain Drip
Sun Veil
Terra Furniture, Inc.
Tropitone Furniture Co.
Universal Gerwin division of Leigh Products, Inc.
Weber-Stephens
Lee L. Woodard Sons, Inc.

Page numbers in *italics* refer to photographs or illustrations.

Have BETTER HOMES AND
GARDENS® magazine deliv-
ered to your door. For informa-
tion, write to: MR. ROBERT
AUSTIN, P.O. BOX 4536, DES
MOINES, IA 50336.